北语对外汉语精版教材

速成汉语基础教程

Chinese Crash Course (Third Edition)

主　编：杨惠元

副主编：韩　梅　游锋华　李德钧

Integrated Textbook

综合课本（第 3 版）

7

北京语言大学出版社
BEIJING LANGUAGE AND CULTURE UNIVERSITY PRESS

图书在版编目（CIP）数据

速成汉语基础教程：综合课本. 7 / 杨惠元主编
. —3版. —北京：北京语言大学出版社, 2021.12
北语对外汉语精版教材
ISBN 978-7-5619-6056-1

Ⅰ. ①速… Ⅱ. ①杨… Ⅲ. ①汉语—对外汉语教学—教材 Ⅳ. ①H195.4

中国版本图书馆CIP数据核字（2021）第248000号

速成汉语基础教程 · 综合课本 7（第 3 版）

SUCHENG HANYU JICHU JIAOCHENG · ZONGHE KEBEN 7 (DI 3 BAN)

排版制作：华伦图文制作中心
责任印制：周 燚

出版发行：北京语言大学出版社
社　　址：北京市海淀区学院路 15 号，100083
网　　址：www.blcup.com
电子信箱：service@blcup.com
电　　话：编辑部　8610-82303395
　　　　　发行部　8610-82303650/3591/3648
　　　　　北语书店　8610-82303653
　　　　　网购咨询　8610-82303908
印　　刷：北京印迪数码科技有限公司

版　　次：1996 年 1 月第 1 版　2007 年 9 月第 2 版　2021 年 12 月第 3 版
印　　次：2021 年 12 月第 1 次印刷
开　　本：787 毫米 × 1092 毫米　1/16　印　张：14.5
字　　数：182 千字
定　　价：72.00 元

PRINTED IN CHINA

第3版前言

《速成汉语基础教程·综合课本》（第3版）是《速成汉语初级教程·综合课本》（北京语言文化大学出版社，1996）和《速成汉语基础教程·综合课本》（北京大学出版社，2007）的修订版。在修订过程中，我们努力保持原教材的优势和特色：

1. 全套8册共出词语3600多个，基本涵盖了外国留学生在中国学习、生活的常用词汇。因此，学习本教程的学生可提高使用汉语进行实际交际的能力。

2. 课文内容实用有趣，学生爱学、易学。原版教材筛选和安排了贴近学生生活的、学了就能用的话题，这样的内容学生喜欢学、愿意学。大部分课文语言风趣幽默，能够引起学生的学习兴趣，激发他们的学习积极性。

3. 语法点的讲解基本采用归纳法。由于课文编写不受语法点的绝对限制，允许冒出新的语法点，所以编写的课文语言自然、流畅。多年的教学经验证明，我们对成人的汉语教学，应先使他们对语言现象有真切的感性认识，然后到一定阶段再进行归纳总结，帮助他们上升到理性认识，这样做符合第二语言教学的规律。

4. 第3版的练习保持了前两版"语音→词语→句型→功能→成段表达→篇章结构→阅读理解"一条龙的练习模式。练习大多紧紧围绕当课的生词、课文和语法点，针对当课的重点和难点，为教师组织课堂教学以及对学生进行语言技能乃至语言交际技能的训练服务。

在广泛征求教材使用者意见的基础上，我们进行了修订，使教材进一步完善。我们替换了内容过时的课文，删去了不常用的生词，增加了使用频率高的新词。为方便教学，我们增加了一些练习，把原有的练习调整为课堂练习和家庭作业两个部分，这样课上课下既分工又合作。我们以课堂练习为主，家庭作业为辅。家庭作业既可以是课堂教学的弹性内容，也可以作为第二天课上复习、检查的内容。

修订这套教材，我们总的指导思想是：以语音、词汇、语法、汉字等语言要素的教学为基础，通过课堂教学，帮助学生把语言要素转化为语言技能，进而转化为语言交际技能。为此，我们提出以下教学建议：

1. 语音是学生语言能力的门面，也是对外汉语教学的难点之一，所以我们保留了语音集中教学的前10课，在其他各课中仍然进行分散的语音训练，希望教师根据学生的发音问题，有选择、有重点、有针对性地进行语音训练。特别是声调的练习，我们特意将“定调音节”的练习延伸到第四册。因为汉语词大部分是双音节词，掌握了双音节的声调，就等于掌握了大部分汉语词的声调。双音节声调搭配总共只有20个，我们选了20个双音节作为定调标准。掌握了这20个双音节的声调，以后学生出现声调错误时，用定调音节提示一下，他们便可自行改正。练习中的“朗读定调音节”在第一册前9课是朗读拼音，第一册第十课以后过渡为朗读汉字。

2. 第一册的重点虽然是语音训练，但教师在突出听说训练的同时，也要重视汉字的认读和书写练习，帮助学生打好汉字基础。第一、二册各课后都附有“汉字表”，为了简明，我们删去了“繁体”一栏（如有必要，另出版繁体字版），保留了笔画笔顺和构成合体字的拆分部件两个部分。

3. 第二册到第八册的重点是词语教学，教师要帮助学生全面掌握好词语的“音、形、义、用”。每课生词表里的生词包括课文中的生词和练习中的生词。按照北语的教学模式，教师应该要求学生课前预习好生词，基本掌握词语的“音”和“义”。课堂练习的重点是词语的“音、义、用”，特别是词语的搭配和活用。词语的“形”可让学生通过家庭作业掌握。

4. 离合词是汉语特有的语言现象，且大多是动词。在前两版中，有的作为词组处理，不标注词性，汉语拼音分写；有的作为词处理，标注动词，汉语拼音连写。本次修订统一作为词，标注词性，汉语拼音连写。因为特殊，学生难于掌握，常常用错，所以在教学中教师要重视离合词的讲练。

5. 本教程是为外国留学生编写的，生词表中有个别生词的拼音标的是变调

（包括轻声），而没有采用《现代汉语词典》（第7版）标注的本调。这样，他们学习和使用起来比较贴近生活。离合词的拼音连写也是基于这一理念。

6. 汉语普通话是以北京语音为标准音，以北方话为基础方言的。我们本着这一原则处理儿化音，根据北京语音在需要儿化的词语后都加了“儿”，以方便学生学习地道的汉语普通话。

7. 语法讲解从结构入手，不追求系统性，力求简单明白，重视语义和语用功能的说明。教师可通过图片、动作、视频等各种直观手段展示语法点，再进行机械练习，最后落实到活用上，使学生置身于语言交际情境中，而不是语法术语和概念中。

8. 课文以话题为中心，为学生提供交际的模式。第一册到第四册的重点是关于学习、生活方面的交际，从第五册开始，话题逐渐向社会交际过渡，增加介绍中国国情、中国人的观念习俗等文化方面的内容。教师要尽量引导学生以课文为范本，说他们自己想说而不会说的话，以此训练学生的汉语思维能力，开发他们的语言潜能，提高交际能力。

9. 本教程逢五逢十的课设计了“功能会话”练习，意在突出“结构与功能相结合”的原则。“功能会话”练习与当课关系不是很紧密，但有一定的概括性。

10. 教师可多采用任务教学法，给学生布置各种交际任务，多组织课堂活动，要求学生使用语言完成交际任务，在交际中学习语言，强化他们学习语言的成就感，激发他们的学习积极性。

编　者

2021年3月

Preface for the Third Edition

Chinese Crash Course: Integrated Textbook (Third Edition) is the revised version of the first edition (*Short Term Intensive Elementary Chinese*, 1996, Beijing Language and Culture University Press) and the second edition (*Speed-up Chinese: Integrated Textbook*, 2007, Peking University Press). It is with the following advantages and features reserved:

1. With a vocabulary over 3,600, the textbooks cover the useful and common vocabulary for foreign students to study and live in China. After learning this course, students are expected to improve their language proficiency in Chinese communication.

2. The materials we used are student-centered, practical and interesting. The unrevised version provided students with materials from daily life, which can be put into practice immediately after class. The language of texts has a fine sense of humor, in which we believe students would be highly motivated in their language acquisition.

3. We apply inductive method to elaborate the grammar points. We have briefly dealt with the most frequently used grammatical rules and explained them in as non-technical a way as possible. New grammar points are not strictly confined to certain text since long-year teaching experience shows that for adult-learners, a general impression for the language will help them form a stronger foundation for their language learning.

4. The training mode of "pronunciation→words and phrases→sentence patterns→function→expressions in paragraph→discourse structure→reading comprehension" keeps unchanged in the third edition. The exercises are closely related to the text. The key grammar points are highlighted in the exercises. It is designed

to assist teachers to organize in-class activities and consolidate the students' in-class acquisition.

We revised the textbooks based on the suggestions of textbook users. Outdated texts were changed, uncommonly used words were deleted, and new frequently used words were added. For the teachers' convenience, we replenished some exercises, and divided the original exercises into in-class exercises and homework. Thus, in-class exercises and homework have cooperation and division, mainly in-class exercises and homework as a supplement. Homework can be used as the flexible content for class teaching, some can be used for reviewing and examining on the second day.

Our guideline for this revision is to integrate phonetics, vocabulary, grammar and Chinese characters into the textbook and by the designed in-class activities, learners are able to transfer what is in the text into daily use and hence they can improve their language skills. To achieve this goal, we propose the following suggestions for teachers:

1. Pronunciation is a key and difficulty for language learners. Accordingly, we reserve the first ten lessons with the focus on pronunciation drills. Pronunciation drills are also distributed in each lesson. We hope that pronunciation drills can be varied according to students' pronunciation problems. Especially tones' practice, we intentionally extended the exercise of "Read aloud the syllables and pay attention to the tones" to the fourth volume. Most of Chinese words are disyllabic, mastering the tones of disyllabic words equates to mastering the tones of most of Chinese words. There are only 20 disyllabic tonal collocations, we selected the 20 syllables as the tone standard. When students make tonal mistakes, the tones of the 20 syllables can be used as a reference for them to correct. "Read aloud the syllables and pay attention to the tones" in lesson 1 to lesson 9 of the first volume is to read aloud the Pinyin, and from lesson 10 of the first volume on, this exercise is gradually transiting to read aloud Chinese characters.

2. Though the first volume focuses on pronunciation drills, Chinese characters

should also be involved in class. Teachers should help the students lay a good foundation of Chinese characters. "Table of Chinese characters' order of strokes" are attached in the first and second volumes. We deleted the column of "traditional Chinese characters" (traditional Chinese characters version can also be published if necessary), and reserved the columns of strokes, order of strokes and components of composite Chinese characters.

3. From the second volume to the eighth volume, the emphasis is on vocabulary. The glossary in each lesson includes new words in the text and exercises. According to "Beiyu mode", students are required to preview the new words before class, and have a basic command of "pronunciation" and "meaning" of the new words. The key of in-class practice is "pronunciation, meaning, use" of the words, especially the collocation and variation of the words. "Form" of the words can be practiced through homework.

4. Segregatory words are special language phenomena in Chinese, most of them are verbs. They are regarded as phrases in the first and second editions, and separately writing of Chinese Pinyin; some of them are regarded as words, parts of speech tagging as verbs, and continuously writing of Chinese Pinyin. In this version, segregatory words are regarded as words, parts of speech tagging as verbs, and continuously writing of Chinese Pinyin. Because its difficulty, teachers should pay attention to the practice of segregatory words for avoiding students' mistakes.

5. The course is compiled for foreign students, so some Pinyin of the new words are marked modified tones (including neutral tone), not the original tone in *Modern Chinese Dictionary (7th Edition)*. Thus, the students can smoothly learn and use Chinese language in daily life. Continuously writing of Chinese Pinyin of segregatory words is also base on the same principle.

6. Beijing pronunciation is the standard pronunciation of Putonghua, and the northern dialect is its basic dialect. According to this principle, we put "er" on the R-pronounced Words, for the students to learn authentic Chinese.

7. Teachers are expected to deal with the most frequently used grammatical rules

and explained them in as non-technical a way as possible. To achieve this, multi-media assistance, like pictures, body language and videos, can be used in class. In this way, students can be immersed in the language rather than lost in the grammatical jungle.

8. The texts are topic-centered and provide students with communication drills. The first volume to the fourth volume is mainly about campus life. From the fifth volume on, more social talks about Chinese culture, customs and ideas are involved. Teachers are expected to focus on the text and try to open students' mouths, improve their language ability and cultivate their language-learning potential.

9. "Functional conversations" is designed for this course every fifth or tenth lesson, with emphasis on "combining the linguistic structure with function". "Functional conversations" might be not closely related to the texts, but it is still a succinct summary.

10. Teachers can apply task-based approach in class and assign different communication tasks to students as much as possible. More in-class activities are strongly suggested. Hence, students are able to learn the language through communication and could be motivated by using the language.

Compilers

March, 2021

第1版前言

《速成汉语初级教程·综合课本》是为短期班零起点的外国学生编写的初级汉语教材（也可供长期班零起点的外国学生使用），教学时间为一个学期（20周），要求学生基本达到国内基础汉语教学一学年所达到的汉语水平。

速成教学时间短，要求高，只有实行“强化 + 科学化”的教学，才能成为最优化的教学。我们认为，速成教学的总体构想应该是：以掌握话题内容为教学的最低目的，以掌握话题模式为教学的最高目的，以掌握语法、功能为实现教学目的的具体措施和根本保障。因此，本教材的总体构想是：以话题为中心，以语法、功能为暗线，以全方位的练习为主体。

教材具体安排如下：共编80课，语音教学贯彻始终。1～10课突出语音（声母、韵母、声调），不涉及语法和功能；11～80课侧重于语法和功能，兼顾语音（难音、难调、重音、语调）。

编写课文时，我们慎重筛选和安排话题。有关生活、学习、交际方面的内容先出，介绍中国国情、中国人观念习俗的文化内容后出。其中，介绍中国国情的内容，以反映社会积极因素为主，但也有个别课文是反映社会消极因素的，避免脱离实际。课文内容的确定，均受一定语法点的制约，但又不捆得过死，注重语言的流畅性和趣味性。课文篇幅逐渐加长，但最长的不超过500字。

这套系列教材共出生词3400多个（专名未计算在内）。注音基本上以中国社会科学院语言研究所词典编辑室所编的《现代汉语词典》为依据，极个别的词参考了《汉语水平词汇与汉字等级大纲》。词性主要参考冯志纯等主编的《新编汉语多功能词典》。每课生词平均43个左右，只要求学生掌握本课重点词语。

语法点的选取主要依据国家对外汉语教学领导小组所编的《汉语水平等

级标准与语法等级大纲》。教材中涉及的语法点，甲级的除少数外全部出齐，乙级的出了大部分，丙级的也选取了一些。我们对少数语法点进行了调整，扩大了趋向补语、结果补语以及主谓谓语句的范围，增加了数量补语。语法难点分散出。对课文中出现的语法点，我们采取分别对待的处理方法：重点的语法点注释略多些，次重点的语法点注释从简，非重点的语法点不加注释，如连动句、兼语句等。语法点不是见一个注一个，基本上采取归纳法，并注意说明使用条件。

这套系列教材共选取100多个功能项目。这些功能项目都是学生最常见、最急用的。对这些功能项目也采取归纳法，而且是在逢五逢十的课中归纳。所归纳的功能项目只具有提示作用，在句型上不求全，教师上课时可根据教学实际情况适当补充。

我们所设计的练习是为教师备课、组织课堂教学、对学生进行技能训练服务的，说到底，是为提高学生的语言交际能力服务的。为此，我们采用了“语音→词语→句型→功能→成段表达→篇章结构→阅读理解”一条龙的练习模式。这些练习为帮助学生打好语音基础、实现从单句表达到成段表达的平稳过渡提供了可靠的保障。

我们的教材编写工作一直是在校领导和国家对外汉语教学领导小组办公室的大力支持下、在院领导的具体指导下、在学院同志的热情帮助下进行的。没有上上下下的通力合作，这套教材是编不出来的。

在教材编写过程中，我们召开过院内专家咨询会、校内专家咨询会，参加过合肥教材问题研讨会。与会专家对我们的教材初稿提出了许多宝贵意见，使我们的修改工作有了准绳。

在编写课文时，我们参考了校内外的有关教材，如韩鉴堂编的《中国文化》、赵洪琴等主编的《汉语写作》、刘德联等编的《趣味汉语》、吴晓露等主编的《说汉语谈文化》、潘兆明主编的《汉语中级听力教程》、吕文珍主编的《五彩的世界》等，从中受益匪浅。

在此，我们谨向有关领导、专家、同行和所有直接或间接帮助过我们的同志表示衷心的感谢。限于水平，教材的缺点和错误在所难免，恳请使用者给予批评指正。

编　者

1995年12月

Preface for the First Edition

Short Term Intensive Elementary Chinese is a Chinese language textbook designed for foreigners at elementary level in short term classes. It can, however, also be used for long term classes. The course covers one semester (20 weeks), students are expected to reach the basic level of one year regular Chinese language learning in China.

Intensive Chinese teaching requires "intensify + science". We think that the basic principle is: the minimum teaching aim is to master the topic contents, the maximum teaching aim is to master the topic mode, and the ultimate aim is to have a good command of grammar and function. In short, the overall design of the textbooks is centered on the topics, grammar and function as inherent clues, and accompanied with various exercises.

The textbooks consist of 80 texts and with pronunciation teaching throughout. Lesson 1 to Lesson 10 deals with pronunciation (initials, finals and tones), and without grammar and function involved. Lesson 11 to Lesson 80 focuses on grammar and function, with pronunciation involved (difficult syllables, tones, stress, and intonation).

Topics are carefully selected for compiling the texts. Topics from daily life are preferable, and then topics related to Chinese culture and customs. Positive aspects of Chinese society are highlighted, however, negative aspects are reserved for authenticity. The texts are restricted by grammar points in some extent, but language's fluency and interest are still pursued. The length of texts is added progressively, no more than 500 words.

The textbooks include over 3,400 words (excluding the proper nouns). Pronunciation is mostly based on *Modern Chinese Dictionary* compiled by dictionary department of Institute of Linguistics at Chinese Academy of Sciences. Some words are based on *Syllabus of Graded Words and Characters for Chinese Proficiency*. Parts of speech are mainly based on *The Newly Compiled Chinese Multiple Functional Dictionary* chiefly compiled by Feng Zhichun and so on. Each text consists of about 43 new words, students are required to have a good command of key words and phrases.

Grammar points are basically selected according to *Chinese Proficiency Graded Standard and Grammar Syllabus* compiled by China National Office for Teaching Chinese as a Foreign Language. Most of grammar points of class-A are included, as well as those of class-B. Grammar points of class-C are also selected. We have adjusted some of the grammar points, and extended the scope of directional complement, resultative complement and clausal predicate sentence, etc. Quantitive complement is also added. We have interpreted the grammar points in different ways: key grammar points are explained in detail, less important grammar points are explained in brief, and non-key grammar points are omitted, for example, sentences with serial verbs and pivotal sentences, etc. The inductive method has been adopted, with explanations to the condition of usage.

Over 100 functional items have been selected in the textbooks, which are useful and practical. These items have been summarized every fifth and tenth lesson. Sentence patterns might not be all covered, teachers can replenish it according to their teaching needs.

The exercises have been designed for teachers' lesson preparation and classroom organization, as well as for students' skills training. In the long run, the exercises aim to improve students' communication skills. We adopted the exercise mode: "pronunciation→words and phrases→sentence patterns→function→expressions in paragraph→discourse structure→reading comprehension". The exercises can be helpful to lay a solid foundation in students' pronunciation and communication skills.

The textbooks have been supported by our university and China National Office for Teaching Chinese as a Foreign Language, as well as our colleagues. Without them, the textbooks cannot be published.

While compiling the textbooks, seminars among experts of our university and college were held. We also attended the conference in Hefei on textbooks. Those experts have given us many helpful suggestions, which are very useful and constructive.

Many textbooks have been used as reference. These books are: *Chinese Culture* (compiled by Han Jiantang), *Chinese Writing* (chiefly compiled by Zhao Hongqin and so on), *Interesting Chinese* (compiled by Liu Delian and so on), *Talking about Chinese Culture* (chiefly compiled by Wu Xiaolu and so on), *Chinese Intermediate Listening Course* (chiefly compiled by Pan Zhaoming), *The Colorful World* (chiefly compiled by Lyu Wenzhen).

We would like to express our sincere thanks to those who have given us direct or indirect help. Because of our limited knowledge, mistakes are inevitable, your suggestions are very much appreciated.

Compilers

December, 1995

第2版前言

《速成汉语基础教程·综合课本》是《速成汉语初级教程·综合课本》的修订版。在修订过程中，我们保持原教材的优势和特色：

1. 全书共出词语3600多个，基本涵盖了《汉语水平词汇与汉字等级大纲》中的甲、乙两级词汇，另有一部分丙级词和超纲词。学完本教程的学生有望通过较高等级的HSK考试。

2. 原教材选取了贴近学生生活、学了就能用的话题，这样的内容学生喜欢学、愿意学。课文语言自然流畅、风趣幽默，能够引起学生的学习兴趣，激发他们的学习积极性。

3. 原教材语法点的讲解基本采用归纳法，课文编写不受语法点的绝对限制，允许冒出新的语法点。多年的教学经验证明，对成年人的汉语教学，首先要使他们对各种语言现象形成真切的感性认识，到一定阶段再进行归纳总结，帮助他们上升到理性认识，这样才符合第二语言教学的规律。

4. 原教材设计的练习大都紧紧围绕课文和当课的语法点，针对当课的重点和难点，能够很好地为教师备课、组织课堂教学、对学生进行语言技能和语言交际技能的训练服务。

原教材使用了10多年，我们也发现一些问题，如有的内容过时，有的练习显得臃肿，有的语法点解释过于烦琐等。这次修订，我们做的主要工作如下：

1. 为学生使用方便，把原教材的四册拆分为八册。本教程是为短期班零起点的外国学生编写的基础汉语教材，原教材80课共四册，每册20课，课本厚，内容多，学生短期内学不完，所以不适合短期班学生选择使用。修订后每册10课，便于教学单位根据学生实际水平灵活选用。学生能够在短期内学完一册课本，也会很有成就感和满足感。

2. 与时俱进，替换了部分课文。原教材中有些过时的内容都已撤换，另外增加了一些新鲜的词语，如“网吧”“上网”“手机”“短信”“数码相机”“MP3”“电子邮件”等等。

3. 压缩了部分练习。原教材的练习丰富有效，但是受教学时间限制，课上不能全部完成，短期班学生又不宜留过多的家庭作业，因此我们精简了练习项目，有些内容移到了与之配套的《速成汉语基础教程·听说课本》中。

4. 精简了语法点的注释。为贯彻“强化词语教学，淡化句法教学”的原则，并且考虑到短期班学生不一定要掌握系统的语法，我们把原教材中过于烦琐的语法注释删去，以便于教师讲解和学生记忆。

修订这套教材，我们总的指导思想是：以语音、词汇、语法、汉字等语言要素的教学为基础，通过课堂教学，帮助学生把语言要素转化为语言技能，进而转化为语言交际技能。为此，我们提出以下教学建议：

1. 由于语音是学生语言能力的门面，也是对外汉语教学的难点之一，我们保留了作为语音集中教学阶段的前10课，同时在各课中仍然进行分散的语音训练，希望教师根据学生的发音问题，有选择、有重点地加强语音训练。

2. 第一册的重点虽然是语音训练，但教师在突出听说训练的同时，也要重视汉字的认读和书写练习，帮助学生打好汉字基础。

3. 第二册到第八册的重点是词语教学。每课生词表里的生词包括课文中的生词和练习中的生词，两部分生词同等重要。在教学中，我们希望教师带领学生完成课后的所有练习，并且重视词语的搭配和活用，帮助学生掌握好词语的“音、形、义、用”。

4. 语法讲解不追求系统性，力求简单明了，从结构入手，重视语义和语用功能的说明。教师可通过图片、动作、视频等各种直观手段展示语法点，再进行机械练习，最后落实到活用上，使学生置身于语言交际的情境中，而不是语法术语和概念中。

5. 课文以话题为中心，为学生提供交际的模式。第一册到第四册的重点是有关学习、生活方面的交际，从第五册开始，话题逐渐向社会交际过渡，增加介绍中国国情、中国人的观念习俗等文化方面的内容。教师要尽量引导学生以课文为范本，说他们自己想说的话，以此训练学生的思维能力，开发他们的语言潜能，提高交际能力。

6. 教师可采用任务教学法，给学生布置各种交际任务，多组织课堂活动，要求学生使用语言完成交际任务，在交际中学习语言，强化他们学习语言的成就感，激发他们的学习积极性。

《速成汉语基础教程·综合课本》(1—8)（第2版）的主编为郭志良和杨惠元。在本教程的修订过程中，张志忠修改了部分插图，赵娅修改了部分语法注释的英文翻译，罗斌翻译了前言。

编　者

2007年2月

Preface for the Second Edition

Speed-up Chinese: Integrated Textbook is the revised version of *Short Term Intensive Elementary Chinese,* with the following advantages and features reserved:

1. With a vocabulary over 3,600, the textbooks cover class-A and class-B words of *Syllabus of Graded Words and Characters for Chinese Proficiency*. Words of class-C and higher are included as well. After learning this course, students are expected to pass the advanced level of HSK.

2. The materials we used are student-centered. The unrevised version provided students with materials from daily life, which can be put into practice immediately after class. In this way, we believe students would be highly motivated in their language acquisition.

3. We apply inductive method to elaborate the grammar points. We have briefly dealt with the most frequently used grammatical rules and explained them in as non-technical a way as possible. New grammar points are not strictly confined to certain text since long-year teaching experience shows that for adult-learners, a general impression for the language will help them form a stronger foundation for their language learning.

4. The exercises are closely related to the text. The key grammar points are highlighted in the exercises. It is designed to assist teachers to organize in-class activities and consolidate the students' in-class acquisition.

The unrevised version has been in use for over ten years. Great changes have been taken place in the world and also in Chinese language. To make the textbook adapt to the changes, we revised the book. For this revision, our main focuses are:

1. For the learners' convenience, we divided the original four volumes into eight.

The revised version targets at short-term beginners. The unrevised version includes 80 lessons distributed in four volumes, with each having 20 lessons. While the revised version has 10 lessons for each volume, it can better suit the needs of short-term beginners.

2. We keep our pace with the times and update the materials. New words, such as Internet café, surf online, cell-phone, text messages are added into the revised version.

3. We removed some of the exercises. The exercises in the unrevised version are abundant. In considering the short learning span, we cut some exercises to suit the short-term learners' needs. A portion of the exercises is transferred to the *Speed-up Chinese: Listening and Speaking*.

4. We simplified the notes and explanations for grammar points. For beginners, emphasis should be put on vocabulary rather than the sentences. We removed some lengthy and complex notes and simplified the explanation to meet the requirements of learners.

Our guideline for the revision is to integrate phonetics, vocabulary, grammar and Chinese characters into the textbook and by the designed in-class activities, learners are able to transfer what is in the text into daily use and hence they can improve their language skills. To achieve this goal, we proposed the following suggestions for teachers:

1. Pronunciation is a key to language learners' learning and communication success outside the classroom. Accordingly, we reserved the first ten lessons with the focus on pronunciation drills. Pronunciation drills are also distributed in each lesson. We hope that teachers can pay continuous attention to students' pronunciation.

2. Though the first volume focuses on pronunciation drills, Chinese characters should also be involved in class. Teachers should help the students lay a good foundation of Chinese characters.

3. From the second volume to the eighth volume, the emphasis is on vocabulary. The glossary in each lesson includes new words in the text and exercises. Teachers

are expected to guide students to finish the exercises. Meanwhile, the collocation and variation of the words should also be emphasized.

4. Teachers are expected to deal with the most frequently used grammatical rules and explained them in as non-technical a way as possible. To achieve this, multi-media assistance, like pictures, body language and videos, can be used in class. In this way, students can be immersed in the language rather than lost in the grammatical jungle.

5. The texts are topic-centered and provided students with communication drills. Volume 1 to volume 5 is mainly about campus life. From volume 5 on, more social talks about Chinese culture, customs and ideas are involved. Teachers are expected to focus on the texts and try to open students' mouths, improve their language ability and cultivate their language-learning potential.

6. Teachers can apply task-based approach in class and assign different communication tasks to students. More in-class activities are strongly suggested. Hence, students are able to learn the language through communication and could be motivated by using the language.

Speed-up Chinese: Integrated Textbook (1—8) (Second Edition) is chiefly compiled by Guo Zhiliang and Yang Huiyuan. Zhang Zhizhong redrew some of the pictures, Zhao Ya revised the English grammar notes and Luo Bin translated the English preface.

Compilers

February, 2007

CONTENTS
目 录

Dì-yī kè
第一课　填　表

一 课文 Text

金汉成希望在初级汉语班的学习结束以后，升入本学院的中级汉语班。他找到办公室的王欢老师，提出了继续学习的想法。王老师说："欢迎你在我院继续学习，不过，按规定，你要办一下儿手续，先填写一张《外国留学生入学申请表》。"说着，他从办公桌的抽屉里拿出一张表，并嘱咐说："填表要用黑笔，表里的主要栏目一定要填写清楚，字要写得工整一些。有的栏目，比如'备注'，就不一定非填不可。你明天交给我，行吗？"金汉成觉得这张表并不复杂，就说："没问题，今天我就把表填好交给您。"

表上的栏目真不少，有姓名、国籍、性别、学历、出生时间和地点、护照号码和有效期、宗教信仰、通信地址、在华留学期限等等。金汉成看了一遍，觉得很容易填，不到半个小时就填好了。当天下午三点，他把表交到了学院办公室。

第二天上午，第一节课的铃声刚响，王欢老师便走进教室，笑着对金汉成说："你填的表我看到了，汉字写得又工整又漂亮。"金汉成心里很高兴，说："谢谢老师！我的汉字写得不太好，您过奖了。"王欢说："可是，你没有填封面上的姓名和国籍。"金汉成拿过表一瞧，果然忘了填写。他红着脸说："对不起，王老师，我太马虎了。"他拿起笔，填好了姓名、国籍，心想，这下子不会再有问题了吧？谁知王老师又说："你不是在'婚否'一栏里画叉儿了吗？可为什么在‘配偶’一栏里有妻子的情况？”“那是我的未婚妻，去年订的婚。”王老师说：“没结婚的不能称为‘配偶’。”“对不起，我以为‘配偶’不但指妻子，还可以指未婚妻呢。”这时，彼得插了一句：“金汉成太着急了吧？”这句话逗得大家都笑了起来。

二 生词 New words

1. 初级	（形）	chūjí	elementary, primary
2. 入	（动）	rù	to enter, to join
3. 中级	（形）	zhōngjí	intermediate
4. 手续	（名）	shǒuxù	procedures
5. 申请	（动）	shēnqǐng	to apply for
6. 栏目	（名）	lánmù	column
7. 工整	（形）	gōngzhěng	nice and neat
8. 备注	（名）	bèizhù	remarks
9. 复杂	（形）	fùzá	complicated
10. 国籍	（名）	guójí	nationality
11. 性别	（名）	xìngbié	gender
12. 有效	（形）	yǒuxiào	effective, valid
13. 宗教	（名）	zōngjiào	religion
14. 信仰	（名）	xìnyǎng	faith, belief
15. 通信	（动）	tōngxìn	to correspond
16. 期限	（名）	qīxiàn	time limit, allotted time
17. 铃声	（名）	língshēng	the ringing sound of a bell
18. 便	（副）	biàn	then
19. 过奖	（动）	guòjiǎng	to overpraise
奖	（动、名）	jiǎng	to praise, to reward; prize
20. 封面	（名）	fēngmiàn	cover (of a book, magazine, etc.)
21. 马虎	（形）	mǎhu	careless
22. 婚否		hūn fǒu	marital status

23. 叉儿	（名）	chār	cross
24. 配偶	（名）	pèi'ǒu	spouse
25. 未婚妻	（名）	wèihūnqī	fiancée
未	（副）	wèi	not
26. 订婚	（动）	dìnghūn	to be engaged
27. 插	（动）	chā	to insert, to interpose
28. 逗	（动）	dòu	to tease

补充词汇 Supplementary words

1. 制定	（动）	zhìdìng	to draw up, to formulate
2. 从事	（动）	cóngshì	to be engaged in, to go in for
3. 专业	（名）	zhuānyè	major, speciality
4. 调查	（动）	diàochá	to investigate, to inquire into
5. 合作	（动）	hézuò	to cooperate, to work together
6. 未来	（形、名）	wèilái	future; in the future
7. 驻	（动）	zhù	to be stationed
8. 外交	（名）	wàijiāo	diplomacy, foreign affairs
9. 教材	（名）	jiàocái	teaching material, course book
10. 资本	（名）	zīběn	capital
11. 名单	（名）	míngdān	name list
12. 选	（动）	xuǎn	to choose, to select
13. 先进	（形）	xiānjìn	advanced
14. 将来	（名）	jiānglái	(in the) future
15. 建设	（动）	jiànshè	to build, to construct
16. 项	（量）	xiàng	(a measure word)
17. 钩儿	（名）	gōur	check mark
18. 至于	（介）	zhìyú	as for, as to

专名 Proper nouns

华	Huá	China

二 课堂练习 Exercises

（一）语音

1. 辨音辨调

shēnqǐng	申请	gōngzhǒng	工种	guóqí	国旗
shénqíng	神情	gōngzhěng	工整	guójí	国籍
zhǐdìng	指定	zōngshì	宗室	zhuānyè	专业
zhìdìng	制定	cóngshì	从事	zhuǎnyè	转业

2. 朗读古诗

登鹳雀楼

[唐]王之涣

白日依山尽，黄河入海流。

欲穷千里目，更上一层楼。

（二）词语

从本课生词表中选择合适的词语填空

（1）我今年在________汉语班，明年去中级汉语班。

（2）山本正汉字写得非常________。

（3）这种药很________，我吃了三次感冒就好了。

（4）丁兰做什么事儿都非常认真，从来不________。

（5）表里所有的________都要填写清楚。

（6）这本书的________设计得很好。

（7）你不是________继续学习吗？办________了吗？

（8）王才说的笑话真________，把所有的人都________笑了。

（9）政府________了有关外国留学生的法律。

（10）警察把事情的经过________清楚了，他们写了一份________报告。

（11）老师是________教育工作的人。

（12）他在大学学的是汉语________。

（13）老师和学生必须互相________，共同努力，才能搞好教学。

（14）我哥哥快结婚了，我________的嫂子是小张的姐姐。

（15）安娜的父亲曾经是美国________华大使。她毕业后也想当________官。

（16）这本________是新出版的，很受学生欢迎。

（17）多学习一些知识就多了一份________，更容易找到工作。

（18）艾米把那束鲜花________在花瓶里了。

（19）小王和小李已经________了，但还没结婚。

（20）这张________怎么没有我的名字？

（21）从小学升________中学不用经过考试。

（22）你________谁当先进教师？

（23）金汉成说："现在学习汉语，是为了________跟中国做生意。"

（24）我们一起________美好的未来。

（三）句型

1. 替换

（1）A：备注必须填吗？

B：不一定非填不可。

这个栏目	填写
今天晚上的舞会	参加
护照	带
他送的礼物	收下
这项活动	搞
我的想法	告诉他
书法课	上
假条儿	写

他的话　　　　　　　　听
这种事儿　　　　　　　调查

（2）A：一定要用黑笔填表吗？

B：不一定非用黑笔填表不可。

用这本教材

买前十排的票

聘请辅导老师

跟他们合作

今天干完这项工作

现在就去办手续

选他当代表

向张老师请假

派他去

两个人住一个房间

2. 判断下列反问句的本意（表示肯定时，在括号里画√；表示否定时，在括号里画×）

（1）不请假，合适吗？　（　　）

（2）换个班学习，还要填申请表吗？　（　　）

（3）这么简单的道理，你也不懂吗？　（　　）

（4）有人打搅你，你高兴吗？　（　　）

（5）我跟谁一起出去的，你不是看见了吗？　（　　）

（6）这么近，还用骑车吗？　（　　）

（7）你不是喜欢这个专业吗？为什么说这个专业不好？　（　　）

（8）他给我们介绍经验！他干过这个工作吗？　（　　）

（9）你不是有个朋友在驻华使馆工作吗？你去请他帮个忙。　（　　）

（10）你不是想当外交官吗？你应该了解各国情况。　（　　）

（11）不学好知识，怎么能建设自己的国家？　（　　）

（12）你不是想学习西方先进的科学技术吗？将来去美国留学吧。

（　　）

（四）每人填一张《入学申请表》，然后就表上的内容练习对话。

四 家庭作业 Homework

（一）阅读

祝你的愿望早日实现

下课的铃声响了。白老师请同学们先别走，她说："为进一步改进我们的教学工作，学校有关方面想了解一下你们的学习情况，并征求你们对教学的意见。为此，我们制定了一份《学习汉语情况调查表》，请同学们认真填写，谢谢大家的帮助与合作！"

表上的调查栏目还真不少，有性别、国籍、年龄、母语、学习目的、对教学和教材的意见等。"学习目的"一栏里共有八项，大内填的是"从事翻译工作"，贝拉在"从事汉语教学"一项上画了钩儿（✓）。艾米选的是"为学习专业做语言准备"，因为她想去北京大学历史系学习。彼得呢，一项也没选。他说："我来中国，除了觉得汉语有意思以外，主要是想亲眼看看中国是个什么样子。至于学习汉语将来干什么，连我自己也不清楚。反正多一张证书，就多了一份资本，将来回国找工作也容易。"白老师说："这么说，你的学习目的应该是为了了解中国。"金汉成选择了三项，大内觉得奇怪，就问他："你不是就想在中国开公司吗？怎么有那么多的学习目的？"金汉成说："我不是非要经商不可。将来万一做生意不成功，我就去当汉语老师或争取做外交官。"贝拉笑着说："未来驻华大使的名单里，说不定会有金先生呢。"大内说："祝你的愿望早日实现，未来的大使先生。"

1. 选择正确答案

（1）下面哪项是短文中没有提到的填表原因？

A. 为了改进教学工作

B. 学校有关方面要了解学生的生活情况

C. 学校有关方面要了解学生的学习情况

D. 征求同学们对教学的意见

（2）表上的调查栏目没提到哪一项？

A. 姓名　　B. 性别

C. 国籍　　D. 年龄

（3）“学习目的”一栏没提到哪一项？.

A. 从事翻译工作　　B. 从事汉语教学

C. 为学习专业做语言准备　　D. 得到毕业证书

（4）金汉成没有选择哪一项？

A. 经商　　B. 从事汉语教学

C. 了解中国　　D. 当外交官

2. 朗读短文

（二）词语

1. 用下列生词至少组成两个短语

（1）初级：________ ________　　（2）手续：________ ________

（3）申请：________ ________　　（4）有效：________ ________

（5）期限：________ ________　　（6）马虎：________ ________

（7）建设：________ ________　　（8）先进：________ ________

（9）制定：________ ________　　（10）调查：________ ________

（11）合作：________ ________　　（12）教材：________ ________

（13）从事：________ ________　　（14）选：________ ________

（15）专业：________ ________　　（16）未来：________ ________

2. 用“至于”完成句子

（1）我只知道这个星期的活动计划，________________。

（2）我们都想去桂林旅行，________________。

（3）我认为事实是这样，________________。

（4）他们来这里主要是调查问题，________________。

（5）小王过生日，我们决定为他点一首歌，________________。

（6）这个月我们办公室必须有一个人出差，________________。

（三）写作

请写一写《我学习汉语的目的》，不少于500字。

五 语法 Grammar

（一）三重否定 Triple negation

三重否定有多种形式，“不一定非……不……”是其中的一种：

There are various triple negations, “不一定非……不……” is one of them:

1. 意思大体上相当于“也可以不……”，强调主观随意性。例如：

By and large, “不一定非……不……” has the same meaning as “也可以不……”, when it is used to stress on subjectivity. E.g.:

（1）“备注”不一定非填不可。

（2）他认为作业不一定非做不可。

2. 意思大体上相当于“最好别……”或“还是不……好”，用于委婉地劝阻。例如：

By and large, “不一定非……不……” has the same meaning as “最好别……” or “还是不……好”, when it is used to tactfully dissuade. E.g.:

（1）雨这么大，你不一定非出门不可。

（2）病还没好，你不一定非去上课不可。

3. 意思大体上相当于“别人／别的事物也可以……”，强调存在多种可行性。例如：

By and large, “不一定非……不……” has the same meaning as “别人/别的事物也可以……”, when it is used to stress on multiple feasibilities. E.g.:

（1）干这种活儿，不一定非你不行。

（2）写字，不一定非用钢笔不可。

（二）反问句（1） Rhetorical questions (1)

无疑而问的疑问句有多种，反问句是其中的一种。反问句在形式上是肯定的，意思就是否定的；在形式上是否定的，意思就是肯定的。它比相应的陈述句语气要重。反问句可以用句尾带“吗”的是非问句的形式。例如：

There are various interrogative sentences without doubt. The rhetorical question is one of them. If it is affirmative in form, it is negative in meaning; and vice versa. The tone of a rhetorical question is stronger than that of its equivalent in a declarative sentence. A rhetorical question can be in the form of a yes-no question with “吗” at the end of the sentence. E.g.:

（1）你觉得我是那种人吗?

（2）你不是在“婚否” 一栏里画叉儿了吗?

六 附录 Appendix

北京语言大学来华留学生入学申请表

BEIJING LANGUAGE AND CULTURE UNIVERSITY

APPLICATION FORM FOR INTERNATIONAL STUDENTS

注意：请认真填写，要求字体工整；也可使用电脑填写。每项都必须填写，不得遗漏。

Very Important: If the form is not filled in on a computer, please write legibly in black or blue ink. Please fill every section of the form.

<table>
<tr><td rowspan="2">护照用名
Name on passport</td><td colspan="3">姓/Family name</td><td rowspan="2">中文名
Chinese name</td><td rowspan="5">照 片
Photo</td></tr>
<tr><td colspan="3">名/Given name</td></tr>
<tr><td>国 籍
Nationality</td><td></td><td>出生地点
Place of birth</td><td colspan="2"></td></tr>
<tr><td>出生日期
Date of birth</td><td colspan="3">年/Y 月/M 日/D</td><td>男 □Male
女 □Female</td></tr>
<tr><td>已婚□Married
未婚□Single</td><td>护照号码
Passport No.</td><td colspan="2"></td><td>宗教
Religion</td></tr>
<tr><td colspan="2">最后学历/Highest education</td><td colspan="2"></td><td>现职业Current or latest occupation</td><td></td></tr>
<tr><td colspan="3">现学校或工作单位/Current or latest school or employer</td><td colspan="3"></td></tr>
<tr><td colspan="2">申请学习时间
Intended program at BLCU</td><td colspan="4">从/from 年/Y 月/M 日/D 到/to 年/Y 月/M 日/D</td></tr>
<tr><td colspan="6">现有汉语水平/Tick the appropriate box to indicate the number of Chinese words you know.
[A] None [B] about 800 [C] about 1500 [D] about 2500 [E] about 3500 [F] about 4000
强化班只限 A、B、C、D四个水平/The Intensive Program is offered only to students in Chinese level A, B, C and D</td></tr>
<tr><td colspan="6">境外永久通信地址/Full non-Chinese permanent postal address:

电话/Tel: 传真/Fax: E-mail:</td></tr>
<tr><td colspan="6">录取通知书接收地址/Address to receive the admission package, if different from above:

电话/Tel: 传真/Fax: E-mail:</td></tr>
<tr><td colspan="6">本人简历（从高中开始）/Curriculum vitae (Starting from high school)
单位（Previous and current educational institute & employer） 时间years attended (from/to) 职务（Position）
________________ From________to________ ________
________________ From________to________ ________</td></tr>
</table>

家庭主要成员/Family members

姓名/Name ____________ 关系/Relation ____________ 电话/Tel. ____________

______________________ ______________ ________________

______________________ ______________ ________________

担保人（担保人可以是父母或亲戚朋友，国籍不限，但学生不能做担保人）Emergency contact (Can be a parent or relative of the applicant, out of China, or in China. Student cannot be the contact)

姓名/Name: ________________________________

国籍/Nationality: ______________ 与本人关系/Relationship to the applicant: ______________

永久通信地址/Permanent Mailing Address: ________________________________

____

单位/Name of employer: ________________________________

电话/Tel: (住宅/home) ______________________ E-mail: ______________________

学生类别/Programs

1. 非学历教育/Non-degree Programs

①短期生（一学期以下）/Short Term Programs (1 semester or less):

□汉语普通班（20学时/周）/Regular Chinese Language course (20hrs/week)

□汉语强化班（30学时/周）/Intensive Chinese Language course (30hrs/week)

□商务汉语（HSK5级），16人开班，不够16人插入其他汉语班学习/Business Chinese Language course (HSK5). Programs need to have at least 16 students. Otherwise, they will be transferred to other classes.

□华裔英才班，16人开班，不够16人插入其他汉语班学习/Elite Class for Ethnic Chinese. Programs need to have at least 16 students. Otherwise, they will be transferred to other classes.

□HSK辅导班4级、5级、6级，16人开班，不够16人插入其他汉语班学习/HSK Preparation Course (HSK 4, HSK 5, HSK6). Programs need to have at least 16 students. Otherwise, they will be transferred to other classes.

②长期生（一至二年）/Long Term Programs (at least 1 academic year)

□汉语/Chinese Language course

□预科班/Chinese Preparatory Course

③高级进修生/Senior Scholar Programs □

④教师进修班/Teacher's Training Programs □

2. 学历教育/Degree courses

①专科生（留学生 学制2年）/College Certificate Programs (International Students 2 years)

□汉语言 Chinese Language

②本科生（留学生 学制4年）/Bachelor programs (International Students 4 years)

□汉语言/Chinese Language ○汉语言/Chinese Language ○汉英双语/Chinese-English Bilingual Studies

○经贸汉语/Economics and trade ○韩汉翻译/Korean-Chinese Translation

□汉语国际教育/Teaching Chinese to Speakers of Other Languages

★ 以下专业与中国学生同班上课，需HSK 5级以上证书（含5级）

The students in the following programs will have classes with Chinese students. The applicants should submit HSK5 (or above).

□汉语言文学/Chinese Language & Literature　□汉语国际教育/Teaching Chinese as a Foreign Language

□新闻学/Journalism　□绘画/Chinese Painting

□书法/Calligraphy　□声乐学/Vocality

□国际政治/International Politics　□人力资源管理/Human Resource Management

□国际事务与国际关系/International Affairs and International Relations

□特殊教育（言语听觉科学方向）/Special Education (Speech and Audition Science)

□外国语（英语、法语、日语、西班牙语、阿拉伯语、朝鲜语（韩国语方向）、德语、意大利语、土耳其语、葡萄牙语、俄语）/Foreign Languages (English, French, Japanese, Spanish, Arabic, Korean, German, Italian, Turkish, Portuguese, Russian)

★ 以下专业与中国学生同班上课，需HSK 5级以上证书（含5级），还需参加各专业组织的数学和英语考试

The students in the following programs will have classes with Chinese students. The applicants should submit HSK5 (or above) and take math and English entrance exams.

□国际经济与贸易/International Economics and Trade　□金融学/Finance　□会计/Accounting

□计算机科学与技术/Computer Science & Technology

□信息管理与信息系统/Information Management and Information Systems

□数字媒体技术/Digital Media Technology

□翻译（英语方向、法语方向）/Translation (Chinese-English or Chinese-French)

我愿意到北京语言大学学习，在校学习期间保证做到下列各项：

1. 遵守中华人民共和国法律。
2. 不从事学习目的以外的活动。
3. 遵守学校的各项规章制度，努力学习。
4. 按时缴纳学校规定的学生应该缴纳的各项费用。

I am willing to study at Beijing Language and Culture University. I pledge the following terms during my study:

1. I will abide by the laws of the People's Republic of China.
2. I will not engage in activities bearing no relation with my academic pursuit in China.
3. I will study industriously and observe all rules and regulations of the University.
4. I will pay all expenses on time.

学生本人签字/Signature of the applicant:　　　　日期/Date:

Dì-èr kè
第二课　你又开了一张空头支票

一　课文 Text

经理宣布了一个好消息：赵林他们开发的新产品顺利通过了专家鉴定！

是啊。半年以来，赵林跟他的同事们一起，天天搞设计做试验，从来没有休息过一个节假日，而且常常加班，半夜才回家。如今，技术革新成功了，新产品开发出来了，赵林的心情怎么能不激动呢？

下午5点钟一下班，赵林就骑上自行车冲出公司的大门，他要赶快回到家，把这个好消息告诉他的妻子。

俗话说，一个成功的男人背后总有一个默默奉献的女人。赵林从心里感谢他的妻子杨静。如果没有杨静的支持，怎么能取得今天的成绩？这些日子，所有的家务活儿，买粮食买菜、洗衣服做饭、送孩子去幼儿园、照顾双方的老人，全都落在她一个人的肩上。想到这儿，赵林加快了速度，平时骑半个小时的路，今天只用了20分钟！

赵林一进家门就大声地喊：“杨静！杨静！”丈夫今天回来得这么早，杨静觉得很奇怪：“哦，你还有回来早的

时候？”“我告诉你个好消息：我们开发的新产品通过了专家的鉴定。”“我当是什么好消息呢，看把你高兴得！”杨静装作不在乎的样子，可心里别提多高兴了。

赵林说：“正好今天发了工资，明天是星期六，上午我陪你逛商场，下午带孩子去动物园。后天……”赵林的话还没说完，电话铃响起来了。杨静拿起话筒：“喂，您哪位？哦，是王秘书哇。您找他有什么事儿？什么？外商要来洽谈业务？听清楚了，明天上午8点，在接待室。”杨静放下话筒，看了赵林一眼：“听见了吧？你又开了一张空头支票。看来，明天还是我一个人带孩子去动物园吧！”

二 生词 New words

1. 空头	（形）	kōngtóu	empty (promise), nominal
空	（形）	kōng	blank, empty
2. 支票	（名）	zhīpiào	check
3. 宣布	（动）	xuānbù	to announce, to declare
4. 开发	（动）	kāifā	to develop, to exploit
5. 通过	（动）	tōngguò	to pass
6. 鉴定	（动）	jiàndìng	to appraisal
7. 试验	（动）	shìyàn	to experiment
8. 加班	（动）	jiābān	to work an extra shift, to work overtime
9. 半夜	（名）	bànyè	midnight

10. 革新	（动）	géxīn	to innovate
11. 冲	（动）	chōng	to rush, to dash
12. 背后	（名）	bèihòu	at the back, behind one's back
13. 默默	（副）	mòmò	silently, quietly
14. 奉献	（动）	fèngxiàn	to contribute
15. 支持	（动）	zhīchí	to support
16. 粮食	（名）	liángshi	food, grain
17. 双方	（名）	shuāngfāng	both sides
18. 落	（动）	luò	to fall
19. 速度	（名）	sùdù	speed
20. 哦	（叹）	ó	(an exclamation)
21. 装作	（动）	zhuāngzuò	to pretend
22. 在乎	（动）	zàihu	to mind, to care about
23. 工资	（名）	gōngzī	salary
24. 商场	（名）	shāngchǎng	store, market
25. 话筒	（名）	huàtǒng	microphone
26. 哦	（叹）	ò	(an exclamation)
27. 秘书	（名）	mìshū	secretary
28. 哇	（助）	wa	(a modal particle)
29. 外商	（名）	wàishāng	foreign tradesman
30. 业务	（名）	yèwù	business, professional work
31. 接待	（动）	jiēdài	to receive

补充词汇 Supplementary words

1. 妇女	（名）	fùnǚ	woman
2. 设备	（名）	shèbèi	equipment, facility
3. 锅	（名）	guō	pot, pan
4. 旅馆	（名）	lǚguǎn	hotel
5. 自动	（形）	zìdòng	automatic
6. 线	（名）	xiàn	line
7. 引进	（动）	yǐnjìn	to import, to introduce
8. 安装	（动）	ānzhuāng	to install
9. 扔	（动）	rēng	to throw, to toss
10. 算账	（动）	suànzhàng	to get even with somebody

11. 重复	（动）	chóngfù	to repeat
12. 处理	（动）	chǔlǐ	to deal with, to handle, to dispose of
13. 分析	（动）	fēnxī	to analyse
14. 祖国	（名）	zǔguó	mother country, homeland, native land
15. 产量	（名）	chǎnliàng	output
16. 人员	（名）	rényuán	staff, personnel

二 课堂练习 Exercises

（一）语音

1. 辨音辨调

jiàndìng	鉴定	bànyè	半夜	shìyàn	试验
jiāndìng	坚定	bànyuè	半月	shíyàn	实验
yìwù	义务	hùlǐ	护理	shèhuì	社会
yèwù	业务	fùnǚ	妇女	shèbèi	设备

2. 学说绕口令

大哥有大锅，
二哥有小锅。
大哥要换二哥的小锅，
二哥不换大哥的大锅。

3. 语调

（1）哦，你还有回来早的时候？
（2）哦，你还有不知道的时候？
（3）哦，你还有不会做的时候？
（4）哦，你还有通不过的时候？

(5) 我当是什么好消息呢，看把你高兴得！

(6) 我当是什么大事呢，看把你急得！

(7) 我当是有多重呢，看把你累得！

(8) 我当是有多少事儿呢，看把你忙得！

（二）词语

从本课生词表中选择合适的词语填空

(1) 小王昨天________从歌厅回来。

(2) 我们这次去杭州旅行住的是小________，很便宜。

(3) 今天刚25号，这个月的________我都花光了。

(4) 你怎么天天________，回来得这么晚？

(5) 山本的嫂子是家庭________，每天买菜做饭，照顾丈夫和孩子。

(6) 这台新________是进口的，那条自动生产线也是从国外________的。

(7) 工人们正在________机器。

(8) 别把纸片________在地上。

(9) 我怎么能________下工作去看电影呢？

(10) 这是一张________支票，银行不付款。

(11) 安娜顺利地________了这次考试。

(12) 这个戒指是不是金的？请你________一下。

(13) 这里是新技术________区，有很多研究项目。

(14) 经理正在跟________洽谈生意。

(15) 这个星期我天天在家里________客人。

(16) 小张和小李在工作上互相________，他们是一对好夫妻。

(17) 这么多家务活儿全________在她一个人的肩上。

(18) 那辆车很________，咱们坐那辆吧。

(19) 我站在你的________，你没看见。

(20) 我只________质量，至于价钱多少我不________。

(21) 老刘很少说话，他总是________地工作。

（22）他的一生都________给了国家的教育事业。

（23）你看，5号运动员________到了最前边。

（24）今天太晚了，明天我再跟你________。

（25）那个孩子骗老师，________肚子疼的样子。

（26）他怎么总是________一个句子？他不会说别的吗？

（27）要________好问题，先得进行调查________。

（28）年轻人要努力学习科学知识，将来更好地建设自己的________。

（三）句型

1. 替换

（1）他们会来的。

调查分析

开发新产品

提高粮食产量

支持你

热情接待你们

参加鉴定会

进行试验

搞技术革新

处理好

通知王秘书

（2）我才不信他的话呢。

相信他

去参加

支持他

去商场

去试验

愿意去

加班

见王秘书

开发这种产品

想理他

2. 给下列陈述句加上合适的句尾语气助词

（1）哦，是王秘书________。

（2）到时候，我会通知你________。

（3）他这是空头支票________。

（4）鉴定会下午两点才开始________。

（5）我们公司也想开发新产品________。

（6）我应该受罚，我骑车带人了________。

（7）他当然会成功了，背后有个默默奉献的妻子________。

（8）今天加班要加到半夜________。

（9）这不说明问题________。

（10）我让他来，他不来________。

四 家庭作业 Homework

（一）阅读

1. 读下面的对话并填空

夫妻对话

赵　林：（敲门）哎，杨静，开门哪！

杨　静：谁呀？半夜三更（sāngēng，late at night）的敲门！

赵　林：连我的________都听不出来了？我是________。

杨　静：是你呀，我还以为是坏人呢，你回来干什么？

赵　林：睡觉呗（bei，a partical）。都半夜了，我还没吃________呢。

杨　静：还没吃________？我才不信呢，经理没请你吃饭？

赵　林：真的没吃饭，骗你不是人。

杨　静：你要是不饿不困就不回家了，是不是？赵大工程师，我这儿是旅馆还是饭店？我是你的保姆（bǎomǔ）还是服务员？

赵　林：杨静！

杨　静：别叫，叫也没有用！今天本旅馆不营业，本饭店也不开张（kāizhāng）！

赵　林：咳，杨静，到月底了，公司里特别忙。那么多工作，我能扔下不管吗？再说，也不是我一个人加班呀，所有的技术人员都刚刚回家，连________也刚刚回家。

杨　静：天天忙，月月忙，你哪天正点下过班？这些日子家里的事儿你问过吗？买粮买菜、洗衣做饭、接送孩子，全成了我的事儿。我不是家庭妇女，我也有自己的工作！

赵　林：杨静，别嚷嚷了，让________听见多不好。以后我多干点儿，不行吗？

杨　静：你还怕人听见？我偏要嚷。经理把你当成大红人，产量上不去找你，自动线坏了找你，设备安装也找你，可怎么不问问你肚子________？

赵　林：杨静，先开开门，咱们屋里说，行吗？

杨　静：想进家门，没那么容易！

赵　林：那我走了。杨静，明天我早点儿________，路上我买菜，晚饭我做。

杨　静：站住！你去哪儿？

赵　林：回________睡觉。

杨　静：你不饿了？

赵　林：饿一顿没________。

杨　静：回来！你以为一走就没事儿啦？没那么简单，进屋来再和你算账……先去吃饭吧，饭菜在电饭锅里热着呢。

2. 根据上下文猜下列词语的意思

（1）保姆——

（2）开张——

（3）月底——

（4）大红人——

3. 回答问题

（1）你觉得赵林这个人怎么样？

（2）你觉得杨静这个人怎么样？

（3）读完对话，你对中国的夫妻关系有了哪些了解？

（二）词语

用下列生词至少组成两个短语

（1）鉴定：________ ________

（2）通过：________ ________

（3）加班：________ ________

（4）奉献：________ ________

（5）支持：________ ________

（6）商场：________ ________

（7）接待：________ ________

（8）宣布：________ ________

（9）算账：________ ________

（10）工资：________ ________

（11）人员：________ ________

（12）自动：________ ________

（13）设备：________ ________

（14）安装：________ ________

（三）句型

把下列反问句改写成相应的陈述句

（1）哦，你还有回来早的时候？

（2）都这么晚了，他还没吃晚饭？

（3）这本教材是你的？你仔细看看！

（4）你工作这么积极，经理没请你吃饭？

（5）你还怕人听见？

（6）这种事儿还能开玩笑？

（7）他半年都没逛过商场？不太可能吧！

（8）不给他加班费，他也不在乎？

（9）你要是不饿不困，就不回家了？

（10）他们那儿是农业大国，还缺粮食？

（四）写作

把课文中的夫妻对话改写成叙述体。

五 语法 Grammar

（一）反问句（2） Rhetorical questions (2)

反问句可以用表示疑问语气的是非问句的形式。例如：

A rhetorical question can be in the form of a yes-no question with an interrogative tone. E.g.:

（1）哦，你还有回来早的时候？

（2）都这么晚了，你还没吃晚饭？

（二）陈述句句尾语气助词 Modal particles at the end of declarative sentences

可用于陈述句句尾的语气助词主要有以下几个：

Modal particles that can be used at the end of declarative sentences mainly are as follows:

1. 语气助词“的”表示肯定。例如：

The modal particle “的”, which is used to express an affirmation. E.g.:

（1）A：我们一起去吧！

B：好的。

（2）他会支持你的。

2. 语气助词“呢”表示指明事实。例如：

The modal particle “呢”, which is used to indicate facts. E.g.:

（1）没关系，我还有呢。

（2）比赛三点才开始呢。

3. 语气助词“啊”（包括变体）表示解释、确认或辩驳。例如：

The modal particle “啊” (including its variants), which is used to indicate an explanation, affirmation and refutation. E.g.:

（1）对不起，我没听清啊。

（2）哦，是王秘书哇！

（3）这并不说明他不孝顺哪。

4. 语气助词“嘛”表示道理浅显或无可奈何。例如：

The modal particle “嘛”, which is used to state a plain reason or to express helplessness. E.g.:

（1）我应该帮助他，他是我的朋友嘛。

（2）我跟他说过了，他不相信嘛。

Dì-sān kè
第三课 王才的求职日记

一 课文 Text

3月2日　　星期四　　小雨

还有几个月就毕业了，我决定从今天起迈出求职的第一步。

首先见的是一位国有企业人事部的面试官。他看着我的简历，先让我做了自我介绍，然后问了我几个问题。他问我为什么想到他们的企业工作，有没有在相关国有企业的实习经验。我不是很了解这家公司，也没有实习过；他又问我父母是干什么的，我说他们都是老师。我不知道这些跟我的求职有什么关系。最后，他和气地对我说："看了你的简历，你符合我们的要求。可是公司最近不缺人，以后有机会再说吧。"我只好离去，冒着小雨返回了学校。

3月10日　　星期五　　阴

我又到一家外国在北京的独资企业面试，见到一位黄头发、蓝眼睛的老板，他用不太流利的汉语问了我的情况。他说："我需要一个翻译，你有能力干好吗？"我说："尽管我的英语水平不高，但我可以试试。"他听了我的话，笑了，说："小伙子，我这儿可不是培训中心，也不是实习场所，等你把英语学好了再来吧。”

回到学校，我向彼得、艾米谈了这次的求职经过，他们说我不会推销自己。唉！推销自己是一门艺术，我哪儿懂这门艺术哇？

3月13日　　　　星期一　　　　晴

我放弃了求职的想法，准备报考研究生。

昨天，我去方云天家玩儿。在饭桌上，谈到毕业后的出路问题，我问方龙老师：“听说咱们学校今年招收研究生，您看我行吗？”没等方老师回答，方云天说：“谁说不行？咱们班里，你年龄最小，学习最好，家里又没困难，与其找个不理想的工作，还不如考研究生呢！”方老师说：“人才应该是高层次、高水平的，只有大学本科的水平恐怕是不够的。那些年纪比你大得多，而且已经有了工作的人还想继续学习，更何况你大学刚刚毕业呢？”

他的话促使我下定决心，报考本校汉语国际教育专业的研究生。

二 生词 New words

1. 求职	（动）	qiúzhí	to apply for a job
求	（动）	qiú	to ask for, to seek
2. 迈	（动）	mài	to step, to stride
3. 步	（名）	bù	step
4. 国有企业		guóyǒu qǐyè	state-owned enterprise
企业	（名）	qǐyè	enterprise, business

5. 面试官	（名）	miànshìguān	interviewer
面试	（动）	miànshì	to interview
6. 简历	（名）	jiǎnlì	curriculum vitae
7. 实习	（动）	shíxí	to practice
8. 最后	（名）	zuìhòu	at last
9. 返	（动）	fǎn	to return
10. 独资	（形）	dúzī	sole proprietorship
独	（副）	dú	only
资金	（名）	zījīn	fund
11. 能力	（名）	nénglì	ability
12. 尽管	（连）	jǐnguǎn	in spite of
13. 培训	（动）	péixùn	to train
14. 推销	（动）	tuīxiāo	to promote sales
15. 唉	（叹）	ài	(an exclamation)
16. 门	（量）	mén	(a measure word)
17. 放弃	（动）	fàngqì	to give up
18. 报考	（动）	bàokǎo	to enter oneself for an examination
19. 出路	（名）	chūlù	way out, outlet
20. 招收	（动）	zhāoshōu	to recruit
21. 与其	（连）	yǔqí	rather than
22. 人才	（名）	réncái	talent, competent personnel
23. 层次	（名）	céngcì	level
24. 本科	（名）	běnkē	undergraduate
25. 恐怕	（副）	kǒngpà	I'm afraid
26. 何况	（连）	hékuàng	let alone
27. 促使	（动）	cùshǐ	to impel, to urge
28. 决心	（名）	juéxīn	determination

补充词汇 Supplementary words

1. 长处	（名）	chángchù	strong points
2. 表现	（动）	biǎoxiàn	to behave
3. 合资	（动）	hézī	to enter into a partnership
4. 骄傲	（形）	jiāo'ào	proud
5. 向往	（动）	xiàngwǎng	to look forward to, to yearn for

6. 过分	（形）	guòfèn	excessive
7. 大胆	（形）	dàdǎn	bold
8. 失败	（动）	shībài	to fail
9. 人际	（形）	rénjì	interpersonal
10. 详细	（形）	xiángxì	detailed
11. 根据	（介）	gēnjù	according to
12. 误解	（动、名）	wùjiě	to misunderstand; misunderstanding
13. 商品	（名）	shāngpǐn	goods, commodity
14. 公关	（名）	gōngguān	public relations
15. 才能	（名）	cáinéng	ability, talent
16. 甚至	（连）	shènzhì	even
17. 招聘	（动）	zhāopìn	to give public notice of a vacancy to be filled
18. ……者		…zhě	used after adjectives or verbs, or after phrases with adjectives or verbs, to indicate people or things with this attribute or doing this action

二 课堂练习 Exercises

（一）语音

1. 辨音辨调

jīdàn	鸡蛋	qīyuè	七月	nénglì	能力
jiēdài	接待	qǐyè	企业	nónglì	农历
tuīxiāo	推销	zhāoshēng	招生	cāngcù	仓促
tuōxiāo	脱销	zhāoshōu	招收	chángchù	长处

2. 学说绕口令

大猫毛短，小猫毛长。

大猫比小猫毛短，小猫比大猫毛长。

（二）词语

1. 从本课生词表中选择合适的词语填空

（1）________求别人不如________自己。

（2）招待会结束以后，他们立刻________回了学校。

（3）这个话剧________了年轻人的爱情生活。

（4）求职者要学会________自己。

（5）有的年轻人喜欢去外国________企业或者中外合资________求职。

（6）这么好的机会你为什么________呢？

（7）我有________做好这个工作。

（8）昨天我们参观了一家公司，这家公司的经理是个难得的________。

（9）王老师专门负责________工程师。

（10）我决定明年________北京大学。

（11）他的学历是大学________，他想今年________研究生。

（12）他们毕业以前要先去医院________，________合格以后才能当医生。

（13）小周太________了，她以为自己比其他同学考得好。

（14）我们单位今年招来了一些高________、高水平的博士研究生。

（15）很多农村的年轻人________城市生活。

（16）这几天我太忙了，明天的宴会我________去不了。

（17）有的人________热情，让人觉得不太舒服。

（18）你们有什么意见可以________地提。

（19）王老师的介绍________我下决心去吐鲁番旅行。

（20）前三次试验都________了，第四次成功了。

（21）每个人都有________和短处。

（22）社会上的________关系比学校里复杂。

（23）你能不能把你们的计划________地谈谈？

（24）________你说的情况，他们一定是误解你了。

（25）他们说的上海话连南方人都听不懂，________外国人呢？

（26）现在市场上的________非常丰富，想买什么就能买什么。

（27）我们公司新来的________经理很有才能。

2. 连线

与其找个不理想的工作，　　　　不如求自己。
与其当翻译，　　　　　　　　　不如坐飞机去。
与其求别人，　　　　　　　　　不如当老师。
与其买这件衣服，　　　　　　　不如去西安旅行。
与其去大同旅行，　　　　　　　不如继续学习。
与其坐火车去，　　　　　　　　不如买那件衣服。

3. 用下列短语填空

甚至不该说的也说　　　　　　甚至不真实
甚至该说的也不说　　　　　　甚至连我
甚至连星期日

（1）说话过分夸张，______________，别人就不相信了。

（2）写文章过分详细，______________，让人不想看；过分简单，______________，又让人看不明白。

（3）他最近非常忙，______________也不能休息。

（4）她说得太快了，______________也听不懂。

（三）句型

1. 替换

（1）你<u>有能力干好</u>吗？

想去求职
想去他们的分公司
也是本科毕业生
愿意去合资企业工作

喜欢搞贸易

想找这家公司的总经理

参加培训

也在独资企业工作

会推销商品

想报考研究生

（2）你大概<u>是第一次来中国</u>吧？

得首先解决这个问题

没实习过

在想毕业后的出路问题

是误解他了

不太了解这里的详细情况

马上就返校

不想放弃这个机会

听说过咱们学校今年招收研究生

了解他的表现

很有这方面的才能

2. 把下列反问句改写成相应的陈述句

（1）在公司工作，哪能不注意人际关系呢？

（2）你根据什么说他不会推销自己？他早找到工作了！

（3）谁说我们公司要招聘新职员？没有的事儿！

（4）那些年纪比你大得多，而且已经有了工作的人还想继续学习，更何况你大学刚刚毕业呢？

（5）当服务员有什么不好？这也是工作需要嘛。

（6）我只是个本科毕业生，算什么人才？

（7）外贸公司有什么可向往的？

（8）这哪儿是他的长处？

(9) 有意见就提，这有什么过分的？

(10) 他的层次高什么？

3. 把下列陈述句改写成特指问形式的反问句

(1) 他并不骄傲。

(2) 他工作不够大胆。

(3) 他算不上人才。

(4) 他的工作表现不太好。

(5) 他介绍得不太详细。

(6) 这点儿钱恐怕不够用。

(7) 他们都不想报考研究生。

(8) 我没有放弃这个想法。

(9) 我这样说并不过分。

(10) 我不想搞外贸。

四 家庭作业 Homework

(一) 阅读

求职是一门艺术

快要毕业的大学生们都想找个理想的工作。但是，他们应该懂得，求职本身就是一门艺术。

过分自信，甚至骄傲，往往不会受用人单位欢迎。而过分谦虚，甚至不敢面对招聘人大胆介绍自己的长处，也往往会引起对方误解。美国有一位研究人际关系的专家曾经说过这样一段话：“生活就是一连串的推销。我们推销商品，推销一项计划，我们也推销自己。会推销自己是一种才能、一种艺术。当你学会推销自己，你几乎可以推销任何有价值的东西。”懂得如何推销自己，是每个想求职的大学生应当学习的一门学问。

某外贸公司是大学生们向往的地方，在公司招聘处，挤满了来求职的大学生，我亲眼看到了两个大学生求职的经过。

一个女大学生，由父母陪着来这里求职，母亲为女儿填写了登记表，招聘处的王先生问："为什么不让你女儿填？"这位母亲回答说："她怕自己填不好。""可是，我们要招聘的是你女儿呀？"事后，王先生对我说："一个读了四年大学的学生，还要父母代自己填表，公司还能靠她去推销产品吗？"

另一位也是女大学生。她来到招聘处前，礼貌地点点头，用英语问："先生，我能用英语介绍自己吗？"王先生愣了一下，随后用英语回答："当然可以，请问你是学什么的？""我是学习国际贸易专业的。""你有哪些特长？""我当过学生干部，可以做公关工作。您看，这是我的简历。"说着，她把简历放在桌子上，中英文各一份。王先生的眼睛亮了起来，他仔细看过简历后说："后天下午3点，你打电话来，我们再详细谈谈，这是我的名片……"

在这次求职中，根据两位大学生的表现，你一定能猜得出来，谁是成功者，谁是失败者。你能说说她们成功和失败的原因吗？

1. 根据上下文说出下列词语的意思

（1）理想的工作——

（2）用人单位——

（3）外贸公司——

（4）特长——

2. 说说两个大学生求职的经过。

3. 谁是成功者？谁是失败者？原因是什么？

（二）词语

1. 用下列生词至少组成两个短语

（1）求：________ ________　　（2）接待：________ ________

（3）推销：________ ________　　（4）放弃：________ ________

（5）报考：________ ________　　（6）过分：________ ________

（7）骄傲：________ ________　　（8）招聘：________ ________

（9）大胆：________ ________　　（10）长处：________ ________

（11）商品：________ ________　　（12）才能：________ ________

（13）外贸：________ ________　　（14）公关：________ ________

（15）详细：________ ________　　（16）表现：________ ________

2. 用“尽管”完成句子

（1）你们有什么意见____。

（2）你们有什么问题____。

（3）需要我帮忙，请____。

（4）____，我们还是去了。

（5）____，但我可以试试。

（6）____________________________________，问题还是没有解决。

（三）写作

写一封应聘汉语翻译工作的求职信，不少于500字。

五 语法 Grammar

（一）反问句（3）　Rhetorical questions (3)

反问句可以用特指问句的形式。这种反问句主要有以下几种：

Rhetorical questions can be in the form of specific questions. This kind of rhetorical questions are mainly as follows:

1. 用“谁”的反问句。例如：

Rhetorical questions with “谁”. E.g.:

（1）东西这么贵，谁买呀？

（2）他是个专家，谁不知道他的名字？

（3）你是负责人，这事儿你不管，谁管？

2. 用“谁说”或“谁说的”的反问句。例如：

Rhetorical questions with “谁说” or “谁说的”. E.g.:

（1）谁说不行？咱们班里，你年龄最小……

（2）谁说的我不同意？

3. 用“什么”的反问句。“什么”可用于名词之前、动词或形容词之后。例如：

Rhetorical questions with “什么”, which can be placed either before a noun or after a verb or an adjective. E.g.:

（1）我真不明白，这些事儿跟我有什么关系呢？

（2）你衣服这么多，还买什么衣服？

（3）我不学这个专业，学什么？

（4）成绩好什么？还不到90分呢！

4. 用“为什么”的反问句。例如：

Rhetorical questions with “为什么”. E.g.:

（1）你是我的朋友，为什么不帮帮我？

（2）这是你的私事，为什么要告诉我？

5. 用“干什么”或“做什么”的反问句。例如：

Rhetorical questions with “干什么” or “做什么”. E.g.:

（1）我又没做过对不起他的事儿，向他道歉干什么？

（2）我又看不懂，买英文小说做什么？

6. 用“有什么”的反问句。例如：

Rhetorical questions with “有什么”. E.g.:

（1）我这样做有什么不对（的）？

（2）这件事儿有什么难办（的）？

（3）这都是些极普通的东西，有什么可买的？

7. 用“怎么”的反问句。例如：

Rhetorical questions with “怎么”. E.g.:

（1）东西这么多，我怎么带？

（2）他是我的同学，我怎么会不认识他？

（3）这种事儿，我怎么敢告诉他呢？

8. 用“哪儿”或“哪里”的反问句。例如：

Rhetorical questions with “哪儿” or “哪里”. E.g.:

（1）到处都这么乱，我哪儿找得到？

（2）他哪里是美国人？他是英国人。

（3）没人告诉我，我哪儿知道？

9. 用“哪”的反问句。例如：

Rhetorical questions with “哪”. E.g.:

（1）学外语嘛，哪个同学没有困难？

（2）说我工作不积极，我问你，我哪天没来上班？

（二）疑问句句尾语气助词　Modal particles at the end of interrogative sentences

可用于疑问句句尾的语气助词主要有以下几个：

Modal particles at the end of interrogative sentences are mainly as follows:

1. 语气助词“吗”用于是非问句和是非问形式的反问句句尾，表示疑问。句中不出现“大概”之类表示揣测的词语。例如：

The modal particle “吗”, which is used at the end of a yes-no question or a rhetorical question in the form of a yes-no question, it can indicate interrogation. Words indicating conjecture such as “大概” and so on cannot be used in this kind of sentences. E.g.:

（1）我需要一个翻译，你有能力干好吗？

（2）您看我行吗？

（3）一个读了四年的大学生，还要父母代自己填表，公司还能靠她去推销产品吗？

2. 语气助词“吧”也用于是非问句和是非问形式的反问句句尾，表示揣测或商量。句中可出现“大概”之类表示揣测的词语。例如：

The modal particle “吧”, which is also used at the end of a yes-no question or a rhetorical question in the form of a yes-no question, it can indicate conjecture or consultation. Words indicating conjecture such as “大概” and so on can be used. E.g.:

（1）你大概是第一次来中国吧？

（2）咱们一起出去走走吧？

（3）我身体不太好，你不会不知道吧？

3. 语气助词“呢”用于疑问句及反问句句尾。例如：

The modal particle “呢”, which is used at the end of interrogative sentences or rhetorical questions. E.g.:

（1）我的词典呢？

（2）他会不会报考研究生呢？

（3）这家公司是独资的呢，还是合资的呢？

（4）我真不明白，这些事儿跟我的求职有什么关系呢？

4. 语气助词“啊”（包括变体）可用于是非问句、特指问句、正反问句、选择问句及各种反问句句尾。例如：

The modal particle “啊” (including its variants), which is used at the end of a yes-no question, a specific question, an A-not-A question, an alternative question and various rhetorical questions. E.g.:

（1）他会不会报考研究生啊?

（2）这件事儿怎么这么难办哪?

（3）这家公司是独资的呀，还是合资的呀?

（4）唉，我哪儿懂这门艺术哇?

Dì-sì kè 第四课　收　获

一 课文 Text

昨天下午，学院举行了一次汉语节目表演。

不到两点，小礼堂里已经坐满了人。刘院长首先讲话。他说："今天的汉语节目表演，是全院师生的一次聚会，也是一次重要的语言实践活动。今年夏天特别热，同学们为学好汉语，不知付出了多少心血，流了多少汗水。现在秋天到了，是收获的时候啦！你们将用精彩的表演汇报学习的收获和成果。最后，祝同学们演出获得成功！"

在热烈的掌声中，表演开始了。同学们演出了丰富多彩的文艺节目，有唱歌的、讲笑话的，有说相声的、演小品的。礼堂里掌声不断，笑声不断，喝彩声更是响成一片。

贝拉、大内、彼得和金汉成演了一个名叫《吃鱼》的小品，受到了大家的欢迎。小品的内容是：丈夫从农贸市场买回一条鲜鱼，价钱非常便宜。妻子怀疑是受污染的鱼，怕吃了

中毒。于是她把鱼肚子切下来，吃了平安无事，妻子这才放心。晚上他们把剩下的鱼吃光了。不料到了半夜，夫妻俩又吐又泻。医生一检查，说他们得了急性肠炎。原来，夏天天热，妻子又没把鱼放进冰箱，一天下来，鱼肉变质了。

表演结束了，经过评选，主持人宣布："小品《吃鱼》荣获一等奖。"在欢呼声中，全班同学和老师向贝拉他们表示祝贺。艾米说："这个节目演得真好哇！你们为全班赢得了荣誉，今天我请客，大家一起庆祝庆祝。你们想吃什么？"

金汉成说："吃什么都行，可就别吃变质的鱼！"

二 生词 New words

1. 收获	（动、名）	shōuhuò	to harvest; gains
2. 心血	（名）	xīnxuè	painstaking effort
3. 汇报	（动）	huìbào	to report, to give an account
4. 成果	（名）	chéngguǒ	achievement
5. 获得	（动）	huòdé	to gain, to acquire
6. 掌声	（名）	zhǎngshēng	applause
掌	（名）	zhǎng	palm
7. 多彩	（形）	duōcǎi	colorful

8. 相声	（名）	xiàngsheng	comic dialogue
9. 喝彩	（动）	hècǎi	to cheer, to acclaim
10. 小品	（名）	xiǎopǐn	short act
11. 污染	（动）	wūrǎn	to pollute
12. 中毒	（动）	zhòngdú	to be poisoned
中	（动）	zhòng	to hit, to be affected by
13. 切	（动）	qiē	to cut, to slice
14. 平安	（形）	píng'ān	safe and sound
15. 剩	（动）	shèng	to remain
16. 不料	（连）	búliào	unexpectedly, to one's surprise
17. 吐	（动）	tù	to spit, to vomit
18. 冰箱	（名）	bīngxiāng	refrigerator
19. 变质	（动）	biànzhì	to go bad, to deteriorate
20. 评选	（动）	píngxuǎn	to choose through public appraisal, to discuss and elect
评	（动）	píng	to comment, to judge
21. 荣获	（动）	rónghuò	to have the honor to get or win
22. 欢呼	（动）	huānhū	to hail, to cheer
23. 荣誉	（名）	róngyù	honor, credit

补充词汇 Supplementary words

1. 担心	（动）	dānxīn	to worry, to feel anxious
2. 会话	（动）	huìhuà	to converse
3. 对话	（动）	duìhuà	to have a dialogue
4. 豆（子）	（名）	dòu(zi)	beans
5. 相反	（形）	xiāngfǎn	contrary
6. 鼓掌	（动）	gǔzhǎng	to applaud
7. 气候	（名）	qìhòu	climate
8. 多么	（副）	duōme	how, what
9. 劲儿	（名）	jìnr	strength, energy
10. 决	（副）	jué	definitely, under any circumstances
11. 癌（症）	（名）	ái(zhèng)	cancer
12. 婚礼	（名）	hūnlǐ	wedding ceremony

13. 娱乐	（动、名）	yúlè	to entertain, to amuse; entertainment, amusement
14. 事故	（名）	shìgù	accident
15. 损失	（动、名）	sǔnshī	to lose; loss
16. 法官	（名）	fǎguān	judge
17. 教堂	（名）	jiàotáng	church, cathedral
18. 左撇子	（名）	zuǒpiězi	left-handed person
19. 之	（助）	zhī	(a structural particle)
20. 恰恰	（副）	qiàqià	just, exactly, precisely
21. 假如	（连）	jiǎrú	if, in case
22. 可见	（连）	kějiàn	it is thus clear that

三 课堂练习 Exercises

（一）语音

1. 辨音辨调

shōuhuò	收获	chéngguō	城郭	dānxīn	担心
shòuhuò	售货	chéngguǒ	成果	dāngxīn	当心
biǎnzhí	贬值	róngyì	容易	huìhuà	会话
biànzhì	变质	róngyù	荣誉	duìhuà	对话

2. 朗读谚语

种瓜得瓜，
种豆得豆。
一分汗水，
一分收获。

3. 语调

(1) 这个节目演得真好哇!

(2) 这个歌儿唱得真好哇!

(3) 这个舞跳得真好哇!

(4) 这幅画儿画得真好哇!

(二) 词语

从本课生词表中选择合适的词语填空

(1) 河水受到________，河里的鱼都死了。

(2) 张老师研究教学法，写了不少文章，取得很多________。

(3) 赵林他们为了开发新产品不知付出了多少________。

(4) ________菜的时候要小心，别切了手。

(5) 秋天是________的季节。

(6) 妈妈从________里拿出来一些饮料。

(7) 那个孩子得了肠炎，又________又泻，被送到了医院。

(8) 祝你一路________!

(9) 老师向同学们宣布："这次考试艾米________全班第一名"。

(10) 他们两个对这件事儿的看法完全________，一个说好，一个说不好。

(11) 校长讲完话以后同学们热烈________。

(12) 在口语课上，老师让同学们做________练习。

(13) 贝拉向老师和全班同学________旅行的经过。

(14) 别________，他不会有危险的。

(15) 这里的________很好，冬天不冷，夏天不热。

(16) 这些孩子乐于助人，________可爱啊!

(17) 他的________真大，能举起100公斤的东西。

(18) 这个秘密我________不告诉别人。

(19) 那两个演员说的________真逗。

(20) 听说母亲得了________，小刘急哭了。

（21）小宋和小林打算旅行结婚，不举行________了。

（22）在晚会上，老师和同学们表演了丰富________的文艺节目。

（23）课后，学校为同学们组织了很多________活动。

（三）句型

1. 替换

（1）<u>同学们</u>不知<u>付出了</u>多少<u>心血</u>。

同学们	流了	汗水
他们	试验了	次
我们	鼓了	掌
我对他	说了	好话
他	做了	好事
他们	取得了	科研成果
这次事故	造成了	经济损失
这个小品	演了	回
这个冰箱	修了	次
他	上了	当

（2）<u>吃什么</u>都行，可就是别<u>吃变质的鱼</u>。

吃什么	吃中毒的鱼
得什么病	得癌症
演什么	让我演法官
去哪儿举行婚礼	去那个地方举行婚礼
跟谁比赛乒乓球	跟左撇子比赛乒乓球
怀疑谁	怀疑我
谈什么	跟我谈这个问题
有什么	有病
缺什么	缺钱
学什么	学如何骗人

2. 给下列感叹句加上合适的句尾语气助词

（1）这个相声说得真好________！

（2）现在是收获的时候________！

（3）这多么危险________！

（4）这里的气候条件多好________！

（5）这多让人担心________！

（6）礼堂里的喝彩声、欢呼声多大________！

（7）他的劲儿多大________！

（8）这个教堂多高________！

（9）马上就要宣布评选结果________！

（10）我的钱剩得不多________！

四 家庭作业 Homework

（一）阅读

左撇子

在一次会话课上，艾米和山本表演了一个小品《左撇子》，艾米演了一个要求离婚的女人，山本演法官。下面是女人和法官的对话。

女　人：因为我发现他并不爱我，我被他骗了。

法　官：是吗？这可不是小问题！他怎么骗你的？

女　人：结婚以前，他对我说："除了你，我决不会爱第二个女人。"可是昨天晚上我才知道，他还喜欢另一个女人。

法　官：这另外一个女人是谁？

女　人：是他母亲。

法　官：说了半天，这另外一个女人是他妈呀！真是笑话！母子之情和夫妻之爱根本是两回事儿嘛！

女　人：不，恰恰相反。昨天晚上我试了试他，我发现他更爱他母亲。

法　官：你怎么知道的？

女　人：我问他："假如我和你妈同时掉进水里，你先救谁？"你猜他怎么回答？

法　官：怎么回答？

女　人："当然先救我母亲啦！因为你会游泳。"

法　官：他说得没错呀！

女　人：我又问他："如果我也不会游泳，你到底先救谁？"他说："我右手救你，左手救我妈。"

法　官：这并不说明他更爱他母亲哪！而且，他说用右手救你，左手救他妈。右手劲儿大，可见他更爱你。

女　人：哪儿啊！他是个左撇子！

法　官：啊？

1. 讨论题

（1）那个要求离婚的女人是被丈夫骗了吗？

（2）那个女人为什么说丈夫更爱他的妈妈？你同意吗？

2. 朗读短文

（二）词语

用下列生词至少组成两个短语

（1）收获：________ ________	（2）汇报：________ ________
（3）成果：________ ________	（4）污染：________ ________
（5）中毒：________ ________	（6）切：________ ________
（7）剩：________ ________	（8）变质：________ ________
（9）评选：________ ________	（10）担心：________ ________
（11）欢呼：________ ________	（12）荣誉：________ ________
（13）婚礼：________ ________	（14）相反：________ ________
（15）损失：________ ________	（16）鼓掌：________ ________

（三）写作

把《左撇子》的对话体改成叙述体。

五 语法 Grammar

（一）强调的表达法（5） The way to express emphasis (5)

表示强调的方法还有一些。

There are some other ways to express emphasis.

1. 用“一定（要）”“必须”“千万”“是”“不知……多少……”“不知怎么……才……”“从来不／没……”“决不／没……”“就（不／没）……”“根本（不／没）……”等词语来表示强调。例如：

“一定(要)”“必须”“千万”“是”“不知……多少……”“不知怎么……才……”“从来不/没……”“决不/没……”“就(不/没)……”and“根本(不/没)……”can be used to express emphasis. E.g.:

（1）我是很喜欢唱歌，可是嗓子不太好。

（2）今年夏天特别热，同学们为学好汉语，不知付出了多少心血，流了多少汗水。

（3）除了你，我决不会爱第二个女人。

（4）母子之情和夫妻之爱根本是两回事儿嘛！

2. 量词、名词重叠形式跟副词“都”搭配使用，表示强调。例如：

Measure words or reduplicated nouns can be used with the adverb “都” to express emphasis. E.g.:

（1）他们个个都很认真。

（2）人人都有一双手。

3. “又……又……”可表示强调。例如：

“又……又……” can be used to express emphasis. E.g.:

（1）不料到了半夜，夫妻俩又吐又泻。

（2）他们又唱歌，又跳舞。

4. 反问句都表示强调。例如：

All of the rhetorical questions can be used to express emphasis. E.g.:

（1）你别听他的，我怎么会不同意呢？

（2）怎么回事儿？你们不是昨天刚结婚吗？

（二）感叹句句尾语气助词　Modal particles at the end of exclamatory sentences

可用于感叹句句尾的语气助词主要是“啊”“了”“啦”。

Modal particles that can be used at the end of exclamatory sentences are mainly “啊” “了” and “啦”.

1. 语气助词“啊”（包括变体）有加强感叹的作用，常与副词“多、多么、真、好”等搭配使用。例如：

The modal particle “啊” (including its variants), which is to strengthen the tone of exclamation, and often used with the adverbs “多” “多么” “真” and “好”. E.g.:

（1）我多高兴啊！

（2）今天天气真好哇！

（3）雨好大呀！

（4）说了半天，这另外一个女人是他妈呀！

2. 语气助词“了”常说成“啦（lɑ）”，是“了（le）”和“啊（ɑ）”的合音，都表示肯定或提醒，常与副词“太”“最”“当然”等搭配使用。例如：

The modal particle “了” is often pronounced as “lɑ”, which is the fusion of “了

(le)" and "啊 (a)", both indicate affirmation or reminding, and usually used with the adverbs "太" "最" and "当然". E.g.:

（1）太好了！

太好啦！

（2）这样最好了！

这样最好啦！

（3）当然先救我母亲了！

当然先救我母亲啦！

（4）下雨了！

下雨啦！

Dì-wǔ kè 第五课 治　病

一 课文 Text

万总经理不是大夫，可是他很会给人治病。

这一天，万总经理把他的两位下级丁经理和于副经理请到家里，说是请他们喝酒。二位经理刚坐下，万总经理就从酒柜里拿出一个很精致的瓷瓶放在他们面前，给每人倒了一杯，说："这是李时珍药酒，又好喝，又能治病，特别是治你们的病很有效。喝吧！"

说实在话，当今的名酒他们二位都喝过不少，可是这种李时珍药酒倒是头一回听说，从来没喝过。丁经理的毛病是好吃，所以肠胃不太好；于副经理的毛病是太懒，症状是四肢无力。他们想，如果这种酒真有效，明天一定多买几瓶。

二位经理先喝了一小口，想慢慢地体会一下酒的味道。丁经理忽然发现这酒味道不对，接着又喝了一大口，不辣、不热、无味。这是水，确定无疑。于副经理也发现这酒味道不对，他看了丁经理一眼，把一杯酒都喝了下去，这的的确确是普普通通的水。

这是怎么回事儿？万总经理不是说给我们治病吗？这普通的水能治什么病？二位经理都这样想，可是谁也没说出来。

不对！按照招待客人的习惯，至少得炒两个菜，哪儿有让客人干喝酒的？一定是万总经理对我平时在下面大吃大喝有意见，用这酒提醒我做人要像水一样清白。丁经理首先悟出了万总经理的用意。想到这儿，他的头上冒出了热汗来。

于副经理也很聪明，他马上想到万总经理一定是对他的工作不满意，认为他成绩平平，跟无味的水一样。厉害呀，难怪别人说万总经理批评人一针见血。想到这儿，他出了一身冷汗。

第二天，万总经理的办公桌上摆着两份极其深刻的检讨书。从此，丁经理的肠胃病好了，于副经理的四肢也有力了。

二 生词 New words

1. 下级	（名）	xiàjí	subordinate
2. 瓷	（名）	cí	porcelain
3. 面前	（名）	miànqián	in front of, before
4. 倒	（动）	dào	to pour
5. 当今	（名）	dāngjīn	nowadays
6. 懒	（形）	lǎn	lazy
7. 症状	（名）	zhèngzhuàng	symptom
8. 肢	（名）	zhī	limb
9. 力	（名）	lì	strength
10. 体会	（动）	tǐhuì	to experience
11. 确定	（形、动）	quèdìng	definite; to determine, to ascertain
12. 无疑	（动）	wúyí	beyond doubt
13. 至少	（副）	zhìshǎo	at least
14. 干	（副）	gān	futilely

15. 大吃大喝		dàchī-dàhē	eat and drink extravagantly
16. 清白	（形）	qīngbái	clean, innocent
17. 悟	（动）	wù	to awaken
18. 用意	（名）	yòngyì	purpose, intention
19. 平	（形）	píng	average, mediocre
20. 难怪	（副）	nánguài	no wonder
21. 一针见血		yìzhēn-jiànxiě	to pierce to the truth with a single pertinent remark
22. 摆	（动）	bǎi	to put, to arrange
23. 极其	（副）	jíqí	extremely
24. 深刻	（形）	shēnkè	deep, profound
25. 检讨书	（名）	jiǎntǎoshū	written self-criticism
检讨	（动）	jiǎntǎo	to make a self-criticism

补充词汇 Supplementary words

1. 书记	（名）	shūjì	secretary
2. 证据	（名）	zhèngjù	evidence, proof, testimony
3. 难受	（形）	nánshòu	to feel ill, to suffer pain
4. 急救车	（名）	jíjiùchē	ambulance
5. 整整	（副）	zhěngzhěng	exactly
6. 投	（形）	tóu	to throw
7. 气	（动）	qì	to get angry
8. 丰盛	（形）	fēngshèng	rich, sumptuous
9. 材料	（名）	cáiliào	material
10. 装模作样		zhuāngmú-zuòyàng	to put on an act
11. 青年	（名）	qīngnián	youth
12. 典礼	（名）	diǎnlǐ	ceremony
13. 记忆	（动）	jìyì	to remember
14. 记者	（名）	jìzhě	reporter, journalist
15. 局长	（名）	júzhǎng	director of a bureau
16. 技术员	（名）	jìshùyuán	technician
17. 呕吐	（动）	ǒutù	to vomit
18. 销毁	（动）	xiāohuǐ	to destroy

19. 粉碎	（形）	fěnsuì	broken
碎	（形）	suì	broken, fragmentary
20. ……犯		…fàn	criminal

专名 Proper nouns

1. 万	Wàn	surname of a person
2. 李时珍	Lí Shízhēn	name of a famous ancient Chinese doctor and pharmaceutist
3. 付	Fù	surname of a person
4. 五粮液	Wǔliángyè	a brand of alcohol

二 课堂练习 Exercises

（一）语音

1. 辨音辨调

shūjí	书籍	jīngzhì	精致	zhèngzhuàn	正传
shūjì	书记	jǐngzhì	景致	zhèngzhuàng	症状
juédìng	决定	jíqí	极其	zhànjù	占据
quèdìng	确定	jīqì	机器	zhèngjù	证据

2. 学说绕口令

十是十，四是四。
十四是十四，
四十是四十。
十四不是四十，
四十也不是十四。

（二）词语

从本课生词表中选择合适的词语填空

(1) 这个工厂的厂长姓付，________姓郑。

(2) 服务员把咖啡放在每个人的________。

(3) 茶几上________着漂亮的茶具。这些茶具都是________的，做得非常精致。

(4) 我完全能________你现在的心情，我一个月没收到信，也很着急。

(5) 小孙感冒了，________是头疼、嗓子疼、鼻子不通、四________无________。

(6) 从这儿到剧场比较远，走路________得用20分钟。

(7) ________贝拉今天这么高兴，原来口语考试她得了第一名。

(8) 小王得了肠炎，又吐又泻，________极了，赶快打电话叫________吧。

(9) 赵林他们在________困难的情况下进行试验，实在不容易。

(10) 那个孩子太________，从来不帮父母做家务。

(11) 这篇文章的内容极其________，人们从中可以________出很多道理。

(12) 今天的练习他做了________两个小时。

(13) 这条路虽然远一点儿，可是路很________，司机们都愿意走这条路。

(14) 到底行还是不行，请你给我一个________的回答。

(15) 考试的时间已经________了，在下个月5号。

(16) 他们今天________喝酒，不吃菜。

(17) 老吴写了一份深刻的________，________了自己不重视安全生产的错误。

(18) 金汉成是一个篮球运动员，他________球很准。

(19) 你说他偷了你的钱包，有什么________？

(20) 听说儿子偷了别人的东西，老张________得要命。

(21) 谢谢您为我们准备了________的晚餐。

(22) 这次试验的________你带来了吗？

（23）他们没有理解老师的________。

（24）你别________了，我们知道这件事儿是你干的。

（25）这些________人非常努力，进步很快。

（26）你怎么没参加毕业________？

（27）艾米的________力很强，这些生词她看一遍就能记住。

（28）那位年轻的记者写了一篇很长的文章，________地批评了某些人大吃大喝的问题。

（三）句型

1. 替换

（1）A：你这是去干什么？

B：我去找 万总经理。

找	于副经理
见	张局长
找	冯技术员
买	五粮液
叫	急救车
写	材料
写	检讨书
练	气功
打	太极拳
做	试验

（2）A：你这是怎么了？

B：我头疼。

四肢无力

想呕吐

太累了

吃多了

是让孩子气的

肚子难受

整夜没睡觉

太困了

感冒了

是打针打的

2. 给下列祈使句加上合适的句尾语气助词

（1）你可不能这么懒________！

（2）出发的日期，你得早点儿确定下来________！

（3）你给大家谈谈体会________！

（4）我们可不能大吃大喝________！

（5）你可要清白地做人________！

（6）这封信，你要早点儿寄出去________！

（7）你要深刻地检讨自己________！

（8）你别装模作样________！

（9）我们可不能让他销毁证据________！

（10）你别干喝酒________！

（四）课堂讨论

1. 万总经理为什么请丁经理和于副经理到家里来喝酒？

2. 丁经理和于副经理喝了无味的“酒”以后，为什么都出汗了？

3. 你认为万总经理给人“治病”的方法好不好？为什么？

（五）功能会话：听后模仿

1. 道歉

（1）A：对不起，我把你的花瓶碰坏了。

B：不要紧。

（2）A：实在抱歉，我今天不能陪你进城了。

B：没关系。

（3）A：我说错了，请原谅。

B：没事儿。

2. 要求尝试

（1）A：我不会修自行车。

B：小王来试试。

（2）A：我的手表不走了。

B：小李修修看。

3. 询问看法

（1）A：上子，你觉得日本人学习汉语哪方面比较容易，哪方面比较困难？

B：阅读方面比较容易，听说方面比较困难。

（2）A：小王，你觉得这两个问题哪个比较简单，哪个比较复杂？

B：我觉得这个问题比较简单，那个比较复杂。

4. 询问动作实现的可能性

（1）A：你四点以前回得来吗？

B：今天工作太多，可能回不来。

（2）A：你六点以前回得来吗？

B：没问题，六点以前回得来。

（3）A：那张桌子那么重，你一个人搬得上去吗？

B：搬得上去。

（4）A：你五点以前买得回来吗？

B：路太远，买不回来。

（5）A：墙上的通知你看得清楚吗？

B：字太小，我看不清楚。

（6）A：这本小说你三天看得完看不完？

B：没问题，看得完。

（7）A：这些啤酒你喝得了喝不了？

B：太多了，我喝不了。

（8）A：这些东西你拿得了拿不了？

B：没问题，拿得了。

（9）A：今天能比赛吗？

B：雨太大了，比赛不了了。

（10）A：骑自行车，一个钟头到得了吗？

B：没问题，到得了。

5. 询问动作发生的时间

（1）A：你是什么时候回来的？

B：我是昨天回来的。

（2）A：他是哪年大学毕业的？

B：他是1995年大学毕业的。

（3）A：云冈石窟开凿于什么时候？

B：云冈石窟开凿于公元5世纪。

（4）A：这个工厂建于什么时候？

B：这个工厂建于1950年。

6. 询问动作发生的方式

（1）A：你们参观得仔细吗？

B：我们一个洞一个洞地参观，参观得很仔细。

（2）A：老师解释得详细吗？

B：老师一个问题一个问题地解释，解释得很详细。

（3）A：你是怎么记住生词的？

B：我一边念，一边造句。

（4）A：你们是怎么去的广州？

B：我们是坐飞机去的广州。

7. 比较

（1）A：这顶帽子跟那顶帽子一样吗？

B：这顶帽子跟那顶帽子一样。

（2）A：这顶帽子跟那顶一样吗？

B：这顶帽子跟那顶不一样。

（3）A：他跟你一样大吗？

B：对，他跟我一样大。

（4）A：他跟你一样大吗？

B：不，他比我大。

（5）A：他跟你一样大吗？

B：不，他比我小得多。

（6）A：他跟你一样大吗？

B：不，他比我小一点儿。

（7）A：他比你大多少？

B：他比我大一岁。

（8）A：你的发音真好！

B：贝拉的发音比我好。

（9）A：你的爱好真多！

B：小王的爱好比我还多。

（10）A：你学习真努力！

B：大内学习比我更努力。

（11）A：你考试太紧张了。

B：丁兰考试比我还紧张。

（12）A：你跑得真快！

B：王才比我跑得还快。

（13）A：你起得真早！

B：方云天比我起得还早。

（14）A：这些小伙子的身体真不错。

B：是啊，他们一个比一个强壮。

(15) A：他的病怎么样了？

B：他的病一天比一天厉害了。

(16) A：你弟弟有你哥哥那么高吗？

B：他们俩一般高。

(17) A：你们学校有北京大学大吗？

B：我们学校没有北京大学大。

(18) A：你们俩谁的发音好？

B：我的发音不如他好。

(19) A：你的爱好很多吧？

B：我的爱好不如你多。

(20) A：这个城市的公共交通怎么样？

B：不太好。坐公共汽车不如骑车快。

(21) A：这些书海运还是空运？

B：空运吧，海运不如空运快。

四 家庭作业 Homework

(一) 阅读

五〇液

大山的女朋友小翠第一次来家里做客，大山的妈妈做了一桌子丰盛的饭菜。大山打开酒柜，指着各种各样的白酒、啤酒和红酒问小翠："你喝什么酒？这些都是我和爸爸喜欢喝的，你自己挑吧！"小翠说："我不会喝酒。""你第一次来我们家吃饭，不喝点儿酒怎么行？"说着，他从酒柜里拿出一瓶五粮液。

正在这时，门铃响了。大山打开门一看，是他们化工研究所的张增，就说："张工程师！"张增问："李局长在家吗？""爸爸还没下班，你找他有事儿吗？"大山回答。张工程师提着两个瓶子走到屋里，说：“局长不在家，我不进去了。明天他不是去北京参加科学技术大会吗？这是专门为他准备的，请你一定交给他。”大山接过瓶子：“啊，五〇液，新产品。交给我跟交给我爸爸一样，你放心好了。”

送走了张增，大山的妈妈问他：“谁来了？”“张工程师送给爸爸的新产品，五〇液。来，尝尝这种酒。”说完，打开瓶子，他先喝了一口。“味道不对！哎呀，肚子难受。这酒……不能喝。”他一边说一边走进厕所呕吐。大山的妈妈看儿子难受的样子又急又气：“这是什么酒？”她拿起一个瓶子摔在地上，瓶子摔得粉碎。“是谁送来的？”“张增，张工程师……”大山一句话没说完，又吐了起来。大山的妈妈说：“小翠，你扶着他，我打电话叫急救车。”

这时，门铃又响了。大山的妈妈打开门：“你是——”“我是张增，局长回来了吗？”“好啊，你来得正好！”“刚才我忘了把这份材料交给大山了……”张增还没说完，大山的妈妈指着他说：“别说了！跟我到公安局去，你这个投毒犯！”“投毒犯？”“你还装模作样？拿毒药当酒的是不是你？”“哎呀，您弄错了！”“错？这是证据！”她拿起另一个瓶子。“啊？那瓶呢？”“摔了，摔碎了！”“你把它还给我！”“还给你？你想销毁证据？”“这是我们刚刚研制出来的化工新产品，请李局长拿到北京进行专家鉴定的，根本不是酒！”“啊？”大山的妈妈不小心把另一个瓶子也摔到地上，摔碎了。

张增跪在地上，看着摔碎的瓶子哭出声来:“我和其他技术员试验了两年，整整50次啊，整整试验了50次啊！”

1. 讨论题

(1) 张增他们研制的新产品为什么叫“五〇液”？

(2) 大山为什么喝这种化工产品？

(3) 大山的妈妈为什么说张增是投毒犯？

2. 复述短文

（二）词语

用下列生词至少组成两个短语

(1) 体会：________ ________　(2) 确定：________ ________

(3) 至少：________ ________　(4) 极其：________ ________

(5) 深刻：________ ________　(6) 检讨：________ ________

(7) 难受：________ ________　(8) 证据：________ ________

(9) 精致：________ ________　(10) 丰盛：________ ________

(11) 粉碎：________ ________　(12) 面前：________ ________

(13) 副：________ ________　(14) 懒：________ ________

(15) 投：________ ________　(16) 摆：________ ________

（三）写作

把叙述体课文《治病》改为对话体。

五 语法 Grammar

（一）祈使句句尾语气助词 Modal particles at the end of imperative sentences

可用于祈使句句尾的语气助词主要有以下几个：

Modal particles used at the end of imperative sentences are mainly as follows:

1. 语气助词“吧”表示委婉的请求、催促、建议、劝阻等。例如：

The modal particle “吧”, which is used to express tactful request, urgent demand, suggestion, dissuasion and so on. E.g.:

（1）快走吧！

（2）喝吧！

（3）这些都是别人送的，你自己挑吧！

（4）别去了吧！

2. 语气助词“啊”（包括变体）表示急切的敦促或诚恳的叮嘱。例如：

The modal particle “啊” (including its variants), which is used to express urgent urge or sincere advice. E.g.:

（1）快走哇！

（2）别紧张啊！

3. 语气助词“啦”表示提醒。例如：

The modal particle “啦”, which is used to call attention. E.g.:

（1）走啦！

（2）上课啦！

（二）主谓谓语句小结　A summary of clausal predicate sentences

汉语里，主谓谓语句种类繁多。

In Chinese, there are various clausal predicate sentences.

一般认为属于主谓谓语句的，有以下几种：

There are usually as follows:

1. “领有者+隶属物+状态”。例如：

“Possessor + subordinate objects + state”. E.g.:

（1）这酒味道不对。

（2）这种病的症状是四肢无力。

2. “整体+部分+状态／动作等”。例如：

“Entirety + part + state/action and so on”. E.g.:

（1）咱们俩谁高？

（2）那些小说有的是为孩子写的。

3. “事物+单位／价钱+价钱／单位”。例如：

“Object + unit/price + price/unit”. E.g.:

（1）苹果一斤三块五。

（2）苹果三块五一斤。

4.“人／动物＋‘这／那’＋‘是’+数量／事物／去向／性质／原因／目的等”。例如：

“People/animal + ‘这/那’ + ‘是’ + quantifier/object/where abouts/quality/reason/purpose and so on”. E.g.:

（1）A：你这是100块。

B：对。

（2）A：你这是美元。

B：对。

（3）A：你这是去哪儿？

B：我去商店。

（4）A：你这是不孝顺父母！

B：没有的事儿。

（5）A：你这是干什么呢？

B：我在写家信。

（6）A：你这是怎么搞的？

B：我是打针打的。

（7）A：你这是为什么？

B：这日子没办法过了！

5.“时间／处所+人／事物+状态”。例如：

“Time/location + people/object + state”. E.g.:

（1）今天天气晴朗。

（2）那里游人很多。

Dì-liù kè
第六课

真得感谢这则广告

一 课文 Text

王欢真苦恼，喝口凉水都长肉。妻子总催着他减肥：“你得想办法减肥了，不然的话，会得心脏病的。”

一个星期天的早晨，他照例打开电视机，一面穿衣服，一面看电视。当他吃力地扣上皮带的最后一个扣眼儿时，一则广告吸引了他。广告说，南方某药厂生产了一种新药叫“减肥灵”，效果显著，男女皆宜。王欢一听，像找到救星一样，高兴得不得了。

吃完早饭，王欢就出门了。他先走进西城的一家药店，问：“您好，这儿有一种叫‘减肥灵’的新药吗？”售货员回答：“对不起，这儿没有。你到别的店看看吧。”王欢立即走出店门。心想，广告里说各大药店都有，这家药店可能小了点儿。

他又跑了好几家，都说没有这种减肥药。有的说：“还没听说过有这种药呢，过两天再来吧。”有

的干脆就是两个字——“没有”。倒是东城一家药店的老售货员对他很热情：“前几天东郊新开了一家大药店，离东郊机场不太远，你去那儿问问。”王欢谢过这位老师傅以后，就往东郊赶去。他想，哪怕跑遍整个城市也要买到“减肥灵”！

就这样，王欢从西城到东城，从市区到郊区，跑了整整一天，问遍了大大小小的药店，最后在东郊的复康药店买到了广告上说的“减肥灵”。天黑的时候，他才拖着沉重的双腿走进家门。

第二天早晨，电视机里又在播“减肥灵”广告，王欢还是一边穿衣服一边听广告。这时，他忽然发现，今天皮带竟一下子扣到倒数第二个扣眼儿里了。“哈哈！”王欢高兴得笑了起来。他拍了拍好像小了些的肚皮，说：“‘减肥灵’灵不灵不知道，昨天一天的活动对减肥倒是挺灵的！我真得感谢这则广告。”

二 生词 New words

1. 则	（量）	zé	(a measure word)
2. 广告	（名）	guǎnggào	advertisement
3. 苦恼	（形）	kǔnǎo	vexed, distressed, troubled
4. 凉	（形）	liáng	cool
5. 不然	（连）	bùrán	otherwise
6. 心脏	（名）	xīnzàng	heart
7. 照例	（副）	zhàolì	as a rule, as usual
8. 一面……一面……		yímiàn…yímiàn…	at the same time, simultaneously
9. 当……时		dāng…shí	while
10. 吃力	（形）	chīlì	strenuous

11. 扣	（动）	kòu	to button up, to fasten
扣眼儿	（名）	kòuyǎnr	buttonhole
12. 皮带	（名）	pídài	leather belt
13. 吸引	（动）	xīyǐn	to attract
14. 显著	（形）	xiǎnzhù	outstanding, striking
15. 皆	（副）	jiē	all
16. 宜		yí	suitable, appropriate
17. 救星	（名）	jiùxīng	savior, liberator
18. 立即	（副）	lìjí	immediately, at once
19. 干脆	（副）	gāncuì	straightforward
20. 哪怕……也／都……		nǎpà… yě/dōu…	even if, even though
21. 拖	（动）	tuō	to pull, to drag
22. 沉重	（形）	chénzhòng	lumbersome
23. 竟	（副）	jìng	unexpectedly, actually
24. 倒数	（动）	dàoshǔ	to count backwards
25. 拍	（动）	pāi	to clap, to pat
26. 肚皮	（名）	dùpí	belly

补充词汇　Supplementary words

1. 限制	（动）	xiànzhì	to limit, to restrict
2. 新式	（形）	xīnshì	new-style, new type
3. 夫人	（名）	fūrén	madam, Mrs.
4. 费	（动）	fèi	to consume
5. 跑步	（动）	pǎobù	to run
6. 议论	（动）	yìlùn	to discuss
7. 粥	（名）	zhōu	porridge
8. 楼梯	（名）	lóutī	stairs
9. 巧克力	（名）	qiǎokèlì	chocolate
10. 踩	（动）	cǎi	to step on
11. 政策	（名）	zhèngcè	policy
12. 灰心	（形）	huīxīn	discouraged
13. 挨	（动）	ái	to endure, to suffer
14. 心疼	（动）	xīnténg	to care for sb., to love dearly

15. 发明	（动、名）	fāmíng	to invent; invention
16. 电梯	（名）	diàntī	lift, elevator
17. 腰	（名）	yāo	waist
18. 对策	（名）	duìcè	countermeasure
19. 睡眠	（名）	shuìmián	sleep
20. 反而	（副）	fǎn'ér	on the contrary
21. 影子	（名）	yǐngzi	shadow

专名　Proper nouns

1. 复康药店	Fùkāng Yàodiàn	Fukang Drugstore
2. 冯明	Féng Míng	name of a person

二　课堂练习　Exercises

（一）语音

1. 辨音辨调

xīnzàng	心脏	chīlì	吃力	xīyǐn	吸引
Xīzàng	西藏	shīlì	失利	xīnyǐng	新颖
xìngzhì	性质	xíngshì	形式	hūrán	忽然
xiànzhì	限制	xīnshì	新式	fūrén	夫人

2. 朗读顺口溜

要想身体好，
晚饭应吃少。
要想不生病，
每天多运动。
精神愉快无烦恼，
早睡早起身体好。

心情舒畅多运动，
身体健康不生病。

（二）词语

1. 从本课生词表中选择合适的词语填空

（1）想不出更好的解决办法，我很________。

（2）现在的电视节目________太多。

（3）小王的听力不太好，他感到学习很________。

（4）太胖的人容易得________病。

（5）一年来，小冯学习努力，进步________。

（6）这个节目________了很多观众。

（7）这种方法省力气，可是________材料。

（8）饭菜已经________了，我给你热热吧。

（9）星期日他________六点起床，然后去操场________。

（10）把衣服扣子________上吧，外边有点儿凉。

（11）他总是在背后________别人。

（12）请打开书，看73页________第5行。

（13）今天早上我只喝了一碗________。

（14）那位老人拖着________的双腿走上楼梯。

（15）孩子们都爱吃________。

（16）在公共汽车上，一个人________了我的脚，他说：“对不起！”我说：“没关系！”

（17）孩子们一边________手，一边唱歌。

（18）下了课，请你________到我的办公室来，我告诉你一个重要的消息。

（19）赵林想，________今天晚上不睡觉，也要把试验做完。

（20）这是国家的________，我们不能改变。

（21）孩子喜欢就让他去学吧，别________他。

（22）别________，坚持下去，一定会成功的！

（23）那个孩子没做作业，________了老师的批评。

（24）单位进口了一些________设备。

（25）女儿累瘦了，妈妈很________她，每天给她做很多好吃的。

（26）电灯是一个叫爱迪生（Àidíshēng）的美国人________的。

（27）这个楼的________又坏了，我们只好爬楼梯了。

（28）张老师的________是护士，在第三医院工作。

（29）我的________今天有点儿疼，我想去医院看看。

（30）这么简单的问题他________回答不出来，真是没想到。

2. 把下列短语扩展成句子

（1）回答得很干脆

（2）做事儿干脆得很

（3）都很干脆

（4）干脆跟你说

（5）干脆不承认

（三）句型

1. 替换

（1）他一面<u>穿衣服</u>，一面<u>看电视</u>。

看电视	穿鞋
拍着肚皮	哈哈大笑
学习	劳动
学习	工作
学习	搞发明
搞设计	搞试验
搞教学	搞科研
搞生产	搞设计

救人	喊
参观工厂	了解生产情况

（2）他一边看广告，一边对我说：“又在骗人！”

给我倒茶	你别为这事儿苦恼
给我倒茶	你可不能灰心哪
喝茶	茶太凉了
吃药	我的心脏不太好
吃药	这种药效果显著
站起身来	大救星来了
站起身来	咱们赶快去机场接总经理
看报	上有政策，下有对策，这怎么行呢
摸着孩子的头	对孩子不能限制得太死啊
喝粥	这粥做得不错嘛

2. 完成句子

（1）他一边捂着肚子，一边____________________。

（2）他一边上楼梯，一边____________________。

（3）他一边吃着巧克力，一边____________________。

（4）他一边慢慢地跑步，一边____________________。

（5）他一边走，一边____________________。

（6）他一面工作，一面____________________。

（7）他一面劳动，一面____________________。

（8）他一面学习，一面____________________。

（9）他一面做生意，一面____________________。

（10）他一面搞外贸工作，一面____________________。

（四）课堂讨论

1. 王欢为什么说“真得感谢这则广告”？

2. 广告说，各大药店都有。为什么王欢跑了好几家都说没有？

四 家庭作业 Homework

（一）阅读

这种方法果然有效

冯明长得又高又胖，他的体重有多少，谁也不知道，只知道他一顿饭至少吃两个菜、三个馒头，还有一碗粥。有一次，他不小心踩了妻子的脚，妻子三天没能上班。

为了帮助冯明减肥，他妻子想了很多办法。先是限制他的饮食和睡眠。妻子规定：一顿饭只能吃一个菜和一个馒头，每天晚睡一个小时，早起一个小时。“上有政策，下有对策”。冯明口袋里总是装着巧克力，饿了就吃一块。过了半年，他的体重不但没减下来，反而又增加了。

后来，妻子给他买了减肥茶，冯明坚持喝了三个月，体重还是老样子。妻子并不灰心，有一天，她对冯明说：“我又想了一个主意，不知道你愿意不愿意试试。”“我听你的，只要能减肥，让我干什么都行。”冯明嘴上这样说，心里却另有打算：只要不让我挨饿，我就听你的。

从那以后，电梯里再也看不见冯明的影子了。他每天上下班都是爬楼梯，而且跑步上下楼。一个朋友在楼道遇见他，跟他开玩笑：“小冯，这14层楼，每天两个来回，滋味怎么样？这种新式减肥方法肯定是夫人发明的。我没说错吧？”冯明笑着回答：“你不知道，老婆心疼我，怕我吃多了消化不了。”

一个月以后，冯明发现这种方法果然有效。他的体重减轻了5公斤，腰带已经扣到倒数第三个扣眼儿了。妻子高兴得不得了，说：“怎么样，这种方法不错吧？又锻炼了身体，又省了钱。”冯明说：“可是费了鞋，明天你去给我买两双旅游鞋吧。”

1. 根据上下文猜下列词语的意思

（1）饮食——

（2）睡眠——

（3）老样子——

（4）上下班——

（5）减轻——

（6）腰带——

（7）省钱——

（8）费鞋——

2. 下列句子的含义是什么？

（1）有一次，他不小心踩了妻子的脚，妻子三天没能上班。

（2）上有政策，下有对策。

（3）冯明嘴上这样说，心里却另有打算。

（4）从那以后，电梯里再也看不见冯明的影子了。

（5）这种新式减肥方法肯定是夫人发明的。

（6）你不知道，老婆心疼我，怕我吃多了消化不了。

3. 用简要的话说出这个故事的主要内容。

（二）词语

1. 用下列生词至少组成两个短语

（1）广告：________ ________　（2）议论：________ ________

（3）政策：________ ________　（4）吃力：________ ________

（5）显著：________ ________　（6）沉重：________ ________

（7）新式：________ ________　（8）立即：________ ________

（9）限制：________ ________　（10）发明：________ ________

(11) 吸引：________ ________　　(12) 灰心：________ ________

(13) 挨：________ ________　　(14) 拍：________ ________

(15) 拖：________ ________　　(16) 凉：________ ________

2. 用“不然”完成句子

(1) 快起来吧，________________________。

(2) 咱们坐出租车去吧，________________________。

(3) 你得参加这次考试，________________________。

(4) 他得了心脏病，得立即送医院，________________________。

(5) 去东北旅行一定要多穿衣服，________________________。

(6) 你们一定要预习听力课的生词，________________________。

3. 用“反而”完成句子

(1) 我原来想，走这条路近，没想到________________。

(2) 我以为把这个消息告诉她，她一定很高兴，________________。

(3) 他每天都来得很早，今天考试，________________。

(4) 现在是春天了，这几天________________。

(5) 又学了半年汉语，他的口语不但没有提高，________________。

(6) 老张说雨快停了，过了一个钟头，雨不但没停，____________。

（三）写作

看图写话《补课》。图中左边的人是北京高德中学的张老师，右边在床上的是她的学生王兰。先回答下面的问题，然后写一段话，不少于500字。

(1) 张老师平时对工作怎么样？

(2) 她跟学生的关系怎么样？

(3) 王兰平时学习怎么样？

(4) 王兰现在怎么了？她在哪儿？

(5) 张老师在做什么？

(6) 张老师是一个怎样的人？

(7) 看了这幅画儿你有什么想法？

五 语法 Grammar

并列复句（1） Coordinate complex sentences (1)

“一边……一边……”与“一面……一面……”可表示同时进行两个动作。例如：

“一边……一边……” and “一面……一面……” can be used to indicate two actions that are in progress simultaneously. E.g.:

（1）他一边拍着肚皮，一边哈哈大笑。

（2）他照例打开电视机，一面穿衣服，一面看电视。

也可表示在进行某个动作时发生了另一个动作。例如：

They can also indicate another action occurs in progress of a certain action. E.g.:

（3）他一边说着，一边坐了下来。

（4）他一面跟我打招呼，一面站了起来。

Dì-qī kè
第七课

一位老华侨的心愿

一 课文 Text

昨天，方龙老师家真热闹。他的舅舅牛思华老先生——一位从美国回来的老华侨带着两个孙子回国探亲。亲人团聚，全家人又高兴又激动。方龙在家里设宴，为舅舅接风。

牛老先生今年80多岁了。他年轻时去了美国，经过艰苦奋斗，创建了公司，而且规模越来越大。事业发展了，牛老先生始终忘不了自己是炎黄子孙。几十年来，这位老华侨不仅思念祖国，还思念祖国的亲人，总想为家乡人民做些事情。三年前，牛老先生曾经回来过一次。那次他是专门来参加母校100周年校庆活动的。为了帮助家庭经济有困难的学生，他向学校捐了50万元人民币。他对校长说："钱不多，就算是我这个老华侨对母校的一点儿心意吧。"

如今，牛老先生已经退休，公司由儿子管理。他有了时间和精力，想回国了却另一桩心愿。牛老先生有两个孙子，一个18岁，一个15岁。两个孙子都是在美国出生的，只会说英语，不会说汉语。为此，牛老先生非常苦恼。他常说："中国人嘛，不会说汉语怎么行？中华民族那么多优秀的文化传统怎么继承？"牛老先生这次回来只有一个目的：送两个孙子回国学习汉语。在宴会上，牛老先生反复强调，华侨的根在中国，华侨的孩子必须学好汉语。他嘱咐方龙，孩子留在这里，对他们一定要严格要求，既要学好汉语，又要学会如何做人，把中国人谦虚、诚实、勤劳、勇敢的传统美德全部继承下来。他们一边吃一边聊，整整聊了一个晚上。

二 生词 New words

1. 华侨	（名）	huáqiáo	overseas Chinese
2. 心愿	（名）	xīnyuàn	wish, aspiration
3. 团聚	（动）	tuánjù	to reunite
4. 设	（动）	shè	to give (a banquet)
5. （家）宴	（名）	(jiā)yàn	(family) dinner
6. 接风	（动）	jiēfēng	to give a dinner for a visitor from afar, to give a reception in honor of a guest from afar
7. 艰苦	（形）	jiānkǔ	arduous, difficult, hard
8. 奋斗	（动）	fèndòu	to strive, to struggle
9. 创建	（动）	chuàngjiàn	to found, to establish
10. 规模	（名）	guīmó	scale, scope
11. 事业	（名）	shìyè	cause, undertaking
12. 始终	（副）	shǐzhōng	from beginning to end, all along, throughout
13. 子孙	（名）	zǐsūn	descendant
14. 思念	（动）	sīniàn	to miss, to think of, to long for
15. 母校	（名）	mǔxiào	one's old school, Alma Mater
16. 周年	（名）	zhōunián	anniversary

17. 校庆	（名）	xiàoqìng	anniversary of the founding of a school or college
18. 捐	（动）	juān	to contribute, to donate
19. 心意	（名）	xīnyì	kindly feelings
20. 退休	（动）	tuìxiū	to retire
21. 管理	（动）	guǎnlǐ	to manage
22. 精力	（名）	jīnglì	energy, vigor
23. 了却	（动）	liǎoquè	to settle, to solve
24. 桩	（量）	zhuāng	(a measure word)
25. 继承	（动）	jìchéng	to inherit
26. 反复	（副）	fǎnfù	repeatedly, again and again
27. 诚实	（形）	chéngshí	honest
28. 勤劳	（形）	qínláo	hardworking, industrious
29. 勇敢	（形）	yǒnggǎn	brave, courageous
30. 美德	（名）	měidé	virtue, moral excellence
31. 全部	（形）	quánbù	whole, entire

补充词汇 Supplementary words

1. 学位	（名）	xuéwèi	academic degree
2. 尽	（动）	jìn	to exhaust
3. 临	（介）	lín	just before, on the point of
4. 送行	（动）	sòngxíng	to see sb. off
5. 打工	（动）	dǎgōng	to do manual work
6. 培养	（动）	péiyǎng	to foster, to develop, to educate
7. 赶	（动）	gǎn	to catch up with, to rush for
8. 悲痛	（形）	bēitòng	sorrowful, grieved
9. 想念	（动）	xiǎngniàn	to miss, to think of
10. 欢喜	（形）	huānxǐ	joyful, happy
11. 凭	（介）	píng	base on
12. 头脑	（名）	tóunǎo	mind
13. 灵活	（形）	línghuó	flexible, nimble
14. 富强	（形）	fùqiáng	prosperous and strong
15. 隆重	（形）	lóngzhòng	grand, solemn, ceremonious
16. 讲述	（动）	jiǎngshù	to tell about, to narrate

专名 Proper nouns

1. 牛思华	Niú Sīhuá	name of a person
2. 炎（帝）	Yán(dì)	(emperor) Yan
3. 黄（帝）	Huáng(dì)	(emperor) Huang
4. 全聚德	Quánjùdé	name of a restaurant

三 课堂练习 Exercises

（一）语音

1. 辨音辨调

qīnrén	亲人	shīyè	失业	jīnglì	精力
qíngrén	情人	shìyè	事业	jìnlì	尽力
chéngshí	诚实	qián bù	前部	xuéwèn	学问
chéngshì	城市	quánbù	全部	xuéwèi	学位

2. 朗读古诗

秋思

[唐]张籍

洛阳城里见秋风，欲作家书意万重。

复恐匆匆说不尽，行人临发又开封。

（二）词语

从本课生词表中选择合适的词语填空

（1）今天，我们在这里设________，为张先生________。

（2）老校长为教育________奋斗了一生。

（3）分别多年的老朋友今天________了。

（4）小英去美国以后嫁给一位________的儿子。

(5) 我有一桩________没有________。

(6) 礼物很轻，但这是我们大家的一片________，请你一定收下。

(7) 结婚五十________是金婚。

(8) 我________不明白他为什么不喜欢他父亲。

(9) 刘教授退休以后________了一所语言学校。

(10) 刚到日本，我们的生活非常________，每天晚上要去公司或饭馆儿________。

(11) 那位老人________死的时候把他要说的话说________了。

(12) 经过________练习，才能记住这些词的意思和用法。

(13) 小刚从来不说假话，他是个________的孩子。

(14) 你是什么时候取得博士________的？

(15) 妈妈把________时间和精力花在孩子身上，她要把孩子________成一个优秀的电影演员。

(16) 快走吧，不然就________不上火车了。

(17) 那位海员的手指接上以后，非常________，现在写字、打字都没有问题。

(18) 谦虚是一种________。

(19) 女儿得了癌症，妈妈的心情十分________。

(20) 那个女孩儿________了父亲的聪明和母亲的美丽。

(21) 这位老华侨始终________祖国和祖国的亲人。

(22) 刚来到中国的时候，艾米非常________她的爸爸和妈妈。

(23) 母亲是个________的人，她每天从早忙到晚。

(24) 他从小就非常________，不怕任何困难。

(25) 听了这个好消息，大家都十分________。

(26) 老牛________着丰富的工作经验当上了经理。

(27) 小张年轻，________灵活，办事又很认真，所以领导很喜欢他。

(28) 公司创建的时候，________很小，现在已经有两千多职员了。

(29) 战争结束以后，这个国家很快________起来了。

(30) 昨天上午学校举行了________的开学典礼。

(31) 玛丽明天回国，今天晚上我们请她吃全聚德的烤鸭，为她________。

(32) 我要为家乡的建设________一份力。

(三) 句型

1. 替换

(1) 他又思念祖国，又思念亲人。

想念亲戚	想念朋友
讲述家庭情况	讲述工作情况
看孩子	做饭
探亲访友	游览名胜古迹
探亲访友	了解家乡的变化
参观母校	为母校捐款
参加校庆活动	为有困难的学生捐款
忙家务	忙工作
当老师	当学生
为家乡办小学	为家乡修路

(2) 他既有能力，又有经验。

有学问	有交际能力
想拿学位	想打工
懂英语	懂法语
爱好文学	爱好艺术
喜欢京剧	喜欢话剧
年轻	热情
诚实	聪明

勤劳	勇敢
紧张	愉快
激动	欢喜

2. 从下列句子中挑选出可变换为“既……又……”和“又是……又是……”格式的句子

(1) 这个人又吹牛，又骗人。

(2) 孩子做错了事儿，他又打又骂。

(3) 他又懂业务，又有事业心。

(4) 这地方又干净，又安静。

(5) 你这样说，又对又不对。

(6) 她见到分别多年的弟弟，心里又高兴，又难过。

(7) 亲人团聚，全家又高兴又激动。

(8) 他又有工作经验，又有工作热情。

(9) 他又可能去颐和园，又可能去故宫。

(10) 他又头脑灵活，又有艰苦奋斗的精神。

(11) 这个工厂规模又大，设备又全。

(12) 这个人又干坏事，又怕别人知道。

四 家庭作业 Homework

(一) 阅读

有钱的出钱，有力的出力

三年前，方龙的舅舅牛思华老先生第一次从美国回来探亲，全家都高兴极了。特别是方龙的妈妈，看见分别多年的弟弟，心情又是激动又是欢喜。她一直拉着弟弟的手问这问那，好像有问不完的问题，有说不尽的话。

牛老先生讲述了他的家庭情况。60多年前他一个人来到美国，一边打工一边上学，大学毕业后考上了研究生，拿到了硕士和博士学位。28岁的时候，他跟一位华侨的女儿结了婚，生了一个儿子。现在，他又有了两个可爱的孙子。全家人住在一起，生活非常幸福。

他还讲了他的工作情况。开始，他在一家美国人开的公司里当高级职员，后来创建了自己的公司。凭着勤劳的双手、灵活的头脑和艰苦奋斗的精神，他的公司发展很快，规模越来越大。这些年来，他非常想念祖国和亲人，可是一直抽不出身来。现在他退休了，公司交给儿子管理，他可以经常回祖国看看了。

牛老先生这次回来，除了探亲，还有一个重要目的。他说："后天是母校100周年校庆，我在网上看到这个消息后就回来了，我要参加这个隆重的庆祝活动。"他还说："一个国家要富强，首先要发展教育，培养高水平的人才。为了帮助家庭经济有困难的学生，我打算捐给母校50万元人民币，表达一下我这个炎黄子孙的一点儿心意。"

听了牛老先生的话，全家人深受感动。方龙说："舅舅讲得真好！发展教育是一个国家的头等大事。我是当老师的，云天毕业后也想当老师。舅舅为发展教育事业出钱，我们为发展教育事业出力。这叫有钱的出钱，有力的出力。"这句话把大家都逗笑了。

1. 回答问题

（1）牛思华先生一共讲了几个问题？请概括说明。

（2）方龙为什么说"舅舅讲得真好"？

（3）"有钱的出钱，有力的出力"是什么意思？

2. 朗读短文

（二）词语

用下列生词至少组成两个短语

（1）接风：________ ________　　（2）艰苦：________ ________

（3）奋斗：________ ________　　（4）创建：________ ________

(5) 事业：________ ________ (6) 始终：________ ________

(7) 心意：________ ________ (8) 精力：________ ________

(9) 了却：________ ________ (10) 继承：________ ________

(11) 反复：________ ________ (12) 诚实：________ ________

(13) 勤劳：________ ________ (14) 勇敢：________ ________

(15) 全部：________ ________ (16) 悲痛：________ ________

(17) 灵活：________ ________ (18) 想念：________ ________

(19) 富强：________ ________ (20) 培养：________ ________

（三）写作

请写一写你回国以后的心愿，不少于500字。

五 语法 Grammar

并列复句（2） Coordinate complex sentences (2)

1. "又……又……"格式可表示多种意义，其中之一是表示两种（或多种）事物、人、动作行为、状态（包括客观事物状态和心理状态，心理状态又包括感觉、情感、看法和想法）、属性、功用、效用、原因、目的、条件、结果等同时存在。例如：

"又……又……" can be used to express various meanings, and one of them is to express simultaneous existence of two (or more) objects, persons, actions, states (including objective state and psychological state, which includes perception, emotion, opinion and idea), properties, functions, effects, reasons, purposes, conditions and results, etc. E.g.:

（1）宴会上，又有鸡，又有鱼。

（2）这孩子又哭又闹。

（3）他又打工，又上学。

（4）他的宿舍又整齐，又干净。

（5）他又激动，又高兴。

（6）他又想逛商店，又想逛书店。

（7）他又会打篮球，又会打乒乓球。

注意：（1）后项语义稍重。（2）形容词或状态动词前边一般不加程度副词。

Points for attention: (1) The latter item in "又……又……" is semantically emphasized. (2) Adverbs of degree cannot be placed before adjectives or state verbs.

2. "既……又……"格式所表示的意义跟"又……又……"格式基本相同，只是一般不用形容词或状态动词的一正一反形式。例如：

"既……又……" has about the same meaning as "又……又……", however, the positive and negative form of adjectives or state verbs usually cannot be used in "既……又……". E.g.:

（1）宴会上，既有鸡，又有鱼。

（2）他既打工，又上学。

（3）他的宿舍既整齐，又干净。

（4）他既激动，又高兴。

（5）他既想逛商店，又想逛书店。

（6）他既会打篮球，又会打乒乓球。

3. "既……也……"格式的限制性条件比"既……又……"格式多，还不能用于矛盾的行为或想法。例如：

There are more restrictions on the usage of "既……也……", compared to "既……又……". "既……也……" cannot be used to connect contradictory actions or ideas. E.g.:

（1）宴会上，既有鸡，也有鱼。

（2）他既打工，也上学。

（3）他的宿舍既整齐，也干净。

（4）他既激动，也高兴。

（5）他既会打篮球，也会打乒乓球。

4．“又是……又是……”格式的适用面比“又……又……”“既……也……”格式窄得多。但是，比“又……又……”“既……又……”“既……也……”格式更强调种类不单一。例如：

There are more restrictions on the usage of “又是……又是……”, compared to “又……又……” “既……也……”. “又是……又是……” lays more emphasis on varieties. E.g.:

（1）宴会上，又是鸡，又是鱼。

（2）这孩子又是哭又是闹。

（3）他又是打工，又是上学。

（4）他又是激动，又是欢喜。

Dì-bā kè
第八课 陪妻子逛商店

一 课文 Text

女人大多数爱逛商店，男人却不一样。星期日，妻子又让老田陪她去买衣服。

他们来到胜利商业街。这条商业街有大商场，也有个体的小商店，一个挨着一个。这些商店主要经营服装、日用百货和工艺品。老田的妻子喜欢来这里买东西，有时候去大商场，有时候去小商店。不过，她更喜欢去小商店，一方面因为小商店的商品价格便宜，一方面因为小商店的商贩热情周到。老田跟妻子相反，妻子越喜欢去的地方，他越不喜欢去。老田本来不想去，犹豫了一下，最后还是同意了。

一开始老田觉得很轻松，他帮妻子挑选、给她出谋划策、询问价钱等等。一个小时过去了，老田的脚步越来越沉重，话也越来越少了。看看妻子，脚步还是那么轻松，话还是那么多。两个小时过去了，老田更累了，吃力地跟在妻子后面走。再看妻子，脚步越来越快，一点儿也不觉得累。三个小时过去了，老田对逛商店完全失去了兴趣，而且眼睛也变得模糊起来。可是妻子呢，兴趣越来越浓，眼睛越来越亮，她站在摊位前边仔细地比较、精心地挑选。

妻子买东西特别挑剔。有的衣服颜色、样子好看，可是长短、肥瘦不合适；有的衣服长短、肥瘦合适，她又觉得颜色、样子不好看。就这样，他们转了一个商店又一个商店，从早上一直到中午，也没买到一件满意的衣服。老田累得实在走不动了，只好站在商店门口，看着妻子一会儿进去，一会儿出来，又进去，又出来……

妻子又进了一家时装店。时间不长，妻子招手让老田进去，她拿着一件时髦的丝绸上衣问老田：“你看这件合适不合适？好看不好看？”老田想早点儿买完早点儿回家，就说：“合适，合适！好看，好看！”妻子又指着另外一件："那件怎么样？""绝对合适！绝对好看！"妻子有点儿生气，说："你呀，什么都合适、好看！买东西得精心挑选、仔细比较，哪儿能这么随随便便呢？"老田说："是啊，当初我就是这样随随便便地挑上你的。你呢，也是这样精心挑选才挑上我的。"

二 生词 New words

1. 多数	（名）	duōshù	majority, most
2. 胜利	（动）	shènglì	to win
3. 商业	（名）	shāngyè	commerce, trade, business
4. 个体	（名）	gètǐ	individual
5. 挨	（动）	āi	to be next to
6. 经营	（动）	jīngyíng	to manage, to run
7. 服装	（名）	fúzhuāng	clothing, dress
8. 百货	（名）	bǎihuò	general merchandise
9. 工艺	（名）	gōngyì	craft
10. 价格	（名）	jiàgé	price
11. 一方面……一方面……		yì fāngmiàn… yì fāngmiàn…	on the one hand...on the other hand...
12. 本来	（副）	běnlái	originally
本	（副）	běn	originally
13. 犹豫	（形）	yóuyù	irresolute
14. 出谋划策		chūmóu-huàcè	to give counsel, to offer advice
15. 询问	（动）	xúnwèn	to inquire, to ask about
16. 脚步	（名）	jiǎobù	step, pace
17. 失去	（动）	shīqù	to lose
18. 模糊	（形）	móhu	vague, indistinct
19. 摊位	（名）	tānwèi	stall, (vendor's) stand
20. 精心	（形）	jīngxīn	elaborate, painstaking
21. 挑剔	（动）	tiāoti	to nitpick
22. 时装	（名）	shízhuāng	fashionable dress
23. 绝对	（副）	juéduì	absolutely, definitely

24. 当初	（名）	dāngchū	at the beginning, in the first place

补充词汇 Supplementary words

1. 精细	（形）	jīngxì	meticulous, fine
2. 顾客	（名）	gùkè	customer
3. 兴旺	（形）	xīngwàng	prosperous, flourishing
4. 新颖	（形）	xīnyǐng	novel
5. 美观	（形）	měiguān	pleasing to the eye, beautiful to look at
6. 款式	（名）	kuǎnshì	style, design
7. 做工	（名）	zuògōng	workmanship
8. 宾至如归		bīnzhì-rúguī	guests feel at home
9. 文明	（形、名）	wénmíng	civilized; civilization
10. 主动	（形）	zhǔdòng	initiative
11. 名贵	（形）	míngguì	rare, famous and precious
12. 改革	（动）	gǎigé	to reform
13. 开放	（动）	kāifàng	to lift a ban, to lift a restriction
14. 繁荣	（形）	fánróng	flourishing, prosperous, booming
15. 打折	（动）	dǎzhé	to sell at a discount
16. 迎	（动）	yíng	to receive, to greet
17. 到……为止		dào…wéizhǐ	up to, till
18. 标签	（名）	biāoqiān	label, tag
19. 花花绿绿	（形）	huāhuālùlù	colorful, brightly colored
20. 畅销	（动）	chàngxiāo	to sell well
21. 模特儿	（名）	mótèr	model
22. 景象	（名）	jǐngxiàng	scene, sight
23. 也许	（副）	yěxǔ	maybe, perhaps

专名 Proper nouns

田	Tián	surname of a person

三 课堂练习 Exercises

（一）语音

1. 辨音辨调

sāngyè	桑叶	shèlì	设立	jīngxì	精细
shāngyè	商业	shènglì	胜利	jīngxīn	精心
gùkè	顾客	xīwàng	希望	yóuyì	游艺
guìkè	贵客	xīngwàng	兴旺	yóuyù	犹豫

2. 朗读下面的儿歌

雪花飘

雪花雪花飘飘，
大地披上白袍。
白袍白袍真好，
大地穿上棉袄。
棉袄棉袄真厚，
太阳出来湿透。
小朋友们拍手，
明年一定丰收。

（二）词语

1. 从本课生词表中选择合适的词语填空

（1）上海队经过努力奋斗，终于取得了________。

（2）这家商店主要________服装和鞋帽。

（3）我________不想去，后来他们都劝我，我只好去了。

（4）我们班的同学________会说英语，只有两个人不会。

（5）近几年，这里新建了许多大商场，成了一个新的________中心。

（6）这些建筑设计________，十分________。

（7）这件衣服的________不错，做工也很________。

（8）这是大商场，不是________小商店。

（9）这些服装是从法国进口的高级________，价钱都很贵。

（10）饭馆儿的墙上有一块牌子，牌子上写着四个大字：“________”。

（11）这些孩子以前对客人没有礼貌，现在变得非常________了。

（12）你________这个城市怎么样？

（13）别________了，赶快决定吧。

（14）总经理打电话________我的意见。

（15）上课的时候，同学们都________回答老师的问题。

（16）在医生和护士的________照顾下，我很快恢复了健康。

（17）艾米花了10000美元买了一幅十分________的中国画儿。

（18）这次机会很难得，千万不要________。

（19）天快黑了，前边的山和树都变得________了。

（20）你现在不同意，________为什么不说？

（21）________经济，对外________，使这里的市场越来越兴旺繁荣。

（22）那位年轻的女售货员说话和气，对________非常热情。

（23）你不是拿不定主意买什么礼物吗？请白老师给你________吧。

2. 从下列词语中选择合适的填空

来自　　选自　　出自　　寄自　　译自

（1）这篇文章________《人民日报》。

（2）我们班有的同学________亚洲，有的________欧洲，有的________美洲。

（3）这封信________上海。

（4）这些工艺品都________那位老人之手。

（5）这个词________德语。

（三）句型

1. 替换

（1）我们一方面要工作，一方面要学习。

要学习	要参加劳动
要学习	要多实践
要努力学习	要注意学习方法
要注意质量	要注意速度
要进行经济建设	要进行精神文明教育
抓产品的质量	抓产品的数量
抓教学	抓科研
搞生产	搞科研
搞改革	搞开放
搞设计	搞试验

（2）他有时候经营服装，有时候经营工艺品。

经商	办工厂
搞贸易	搞生产
办合资企业	办独资企业
与外商洽谈业务	办展览
吃中餐	吃西餐
去参观	去旅游
住朋友家	住宾馆
喝葡萄酒	喝白酒
看中国电影	看外国电影
写小说	写诗

（3）妻子一会儿进去，一会儿出来。

小王	上去	下来
这孩子	哭	笑
贝拉病了	觉得冷	觉得热

这儿的天气	晴	阴
他	说去	说不去
她	要吃点心	要吃水果

2. 完成句子

（1）学习外语，一方面要________，一方面要________。

（2）记忆生词，一方面要________，一方面要________。

（3）外出旅游，一方面要________，一方面要________。

（4）买东西，一方面要________，一方面要________。

（5）星期天，他有时候________，有时候________。

（6）这几天，他有时候________，有时候________。

（7）这几个月，他有时候________，有时候________。

（8）这几年，他有时候________，有时候________。

（9）这孩子好动，一会儿________，一会儿________。

（10）他感冒了，一会儿________，一会儿________。

（11）他没有一定的主意，一会儿________，一会儿________。

（12）那里的天气不正常，一会儿________，一会儿________。

四 家庭作业 Homework

（一）阅读

打 折

新年快到了，玛丽听说各大商场和超市都在打折，就约了好朋友丁兰一起到学校附近的一家超市买东西。这家超市的服务员都经过专门的培训，他们对顾客总是笑脸相迎，热情主动地向顾客推销商品，直到顾客满意为止。有的服务员还能说一口流利的英语，玛丽每次来到这里都有一种宾至如归的感觉。

今天超市里真热闹，买东西的人特别多，到处充满着节日的气氛。人们都在忙着买年货，准备过年。玛丽她们赶快推了一个手推车向里边走。

玛丽发现有些商品原来的标签上面又贴了一张黄纸片儿，纸上用红笔写着另外一个价格。

“这是什么意思啊？也许新年到了就把价格写成红色的吧？”玛丽指着标签问丁兰。

丁兰一听就笑了：“才不是呢。这就是打折啊，黄标签上的价格比原来的便宜。”

“噢！”玛丽翻开黄标签看了一眼原来的价钱，“还真是便宜了。我去看看有没有打折的饺子。”

玛丽看到水饺柜台也有黄色的标签，写着“8折”。“这太便宜了吧？”玛丽有点儿不敢相信地说，“原价是12块钱一斤，现在只需要两块多钱！”

“不会吧。哪儿能那么便宜？”听到玛丽的话，丁兰也走过来看价钱。

玛丽指着8折的标签说：“8折是80% OFF的意思，原价12块钱，现价不是两块多吗？”

丁兰这才明白是玛丽理解错了。“汉语的8折是原价的80%，是英语的20% OFF的意思。”“啊，这就对了。原价12块，打折以后9块6。”玛丽买了她爱吃的三鲜馅儿的、猪肉大葱馅儿的、鸡蛋韭菜馅儿的三种饺子。

玛丽还想买衣服。她们看到货架上花花绿绿的男女时装，不仅颜色漂亮，而且款式新颖、做工精细，这些服装都很畅销。玛丽买了一件丝绸上衣，原价240块，打7折后168块。丁兰说：“这件上衣穿在你身上，别人一定以为是名贵的高级时装。你跟服装模特儿似的，能拉不少回头客呢。”“是吗？那应该给我打3折啊！”

从超市出来，玛丽有点儿累，但是她很开心。这不仅仅因为买到了爱吃的饺子、好看的衣服，又学会了汉语“打折”这个词的意思和用法；更重要的是她看到了北京商业兴旺繁荣的景象，体会到中国经济发展给老百姓带来的实实在在的好处。

1. 根据上下文猜下列词语的意思

（1）年货——

（2）手推车——

（3）原价——

（4）回头客——

（5）用法——

（6）实实在在——

2. 回答问题

（1）玛丽为什么喜欢去学校附近的超市买东西？

（2）举例说明汉语的“8折”跟英语的“80% OFF”有什么不同？

（3）玛丽为什么说：“是吗？那应该给我打3折啊！”

（4）买完东西玛丽为什么觉得很开心？

3. 用自己的话叙述玛丽去超市买东西的经过

（二）词语

1. 用下列生词至少组成两个短语

（1）本来：________ ________	（2）多数：________ ________
（3）胜利：________ ________	（4）经营：________ ________
（5）美观：________ ________	（6）和气：________ ________
（7）文明：________ ________	（8）精心：________ ________
（9）绝对：________ ________	（10）繁荣：________ ________
（11）改革：________ ________	（12）询问：________ ________

(13) 失去：________ ________　　(14) 也许：________ ________

(15) 主动：________ ________　　(16) 犹豫：________ ________

2. 用“繁荣”完成句子

(1) 我们的国家越来越________富强了。

(2) 改革开放以后，市场经济更加________了。

(3) 我的故乡变得更________、更美丽了。

(4) 这个城市优美的环境、________给我留下了深刻的印象。

(5) 我们要努力________，提高人民的生活水平。

3. 用“也许”改写句子

(1) 天这么晚了，她可能不来了。

(2) 我们很多年没有联系，恐怕他早把我忘了。

(3) 金汉成大概明年暑假回国。

(4) 走这条路可能近一点儿。

(5) 你去帮他恐怕更好一点儿。

(三) 写作

请写一次在中国买东西的经历，不少于500字。

五 语法 Grammar

并列复句（3）　Coordinate complex sentences (3)

1. “一方面……一方面……”表示两个（或两个以上）动作、原因、目的、条件或结果同时并存。例如：

“一方面……一方面……” indicates simultaneous existence of two (or more) actions, reasons, purposes, conditions or results. E.g.:

（1）他们一方面学习，一方面劳动。

（2）人们喜欢来“OK”街买东西，一方面因为这儿的商品吸引人，价钱比较便宜；一方面因为这里的商贩热情周到。

（3）这里的自然条件不错，一方面果树多，一方面交通方便，应该可以富起来。

（4）逛逛“OK”街，一方面可以看到北京商业兴旺繁荣的景象，一方面可以了解中国改革开放的成果。

2.“有时候……有时候……”表示两个（或两个以上）的动作或状态在不时变化。例如：

“有时候……有时候……” indicates that two (or more) actions or states change from time to time. E.g.:

（1）星期天，他有时候进城买东西，有时候去逛公园。

（2）她对顾客，有时候很热情，有时候不太热情。

3.“一会儿……一会儿……”表示两个动作或状态交替变化。例如：

“一会儿……一会儿……” indicates that two actions or states change alternately. E.g.:

（1）这孩子一会儿哭，一会儿笑。

（2）他一会儿觉得冷，一会儿觉得热，可能是感冒了。

Dì-jiǔ kè 第九课 故乡的小河

一 课文 Text

王欢有八年没回故乡了。八年前的一个暑假，他回到了故乡。

王欢的老家在山东的一个农村，村边有一条小河。王欢小时候每年夏天都去那里游泳、钓鱼，他是喝这条河的水长大的。

回到家的那天，王欢顾不上休息，就向小河走去。走着走着，他闻到一股浓浓的臭味儿。走近一看，河里没有了清清的流水，只有黑色的污水在流动。别说鱼虾了，就连青蛙也见不到一只了，王欢实在不敢相信自己的眼睛。天哪，这就是从前那条美丽的清水河吗？

乡亲们告诉王欢：河的上游建起了好几个造纸厂，废水全往河里流。结果，这个县的工业收入增加了，农业却落后了。不但粮食减产了，而且连老百姓喝水都有了困难。老人们生气地说："这样下去，子孙后代会骂死我们的！"

八年后的这一天，王欢去县城看望了他的老同学——一位刚上任的县长。谈到河水污染问题，县长说："保护环境是百年大计，也是千年大计，不能只顾眼前利益，不顾长远利益。我们这几年彻底治

理了这条河。宁可把河边的工厂都关了，也要为子孙后代留下一条清水河。你放心吧，这次你来探亲，咱俩可以一起去游泳、钓鱼啦！”

回北京以前，王欢又来到河边，向小河告别，他发现这里是绿水青山了。这位新县长的话已经变成了现实。

二 生词 New words

1. 故乡	（名）	gùxiāng	hometown, native place
2. 暑假	（名）	shǔjià	summer vacation
3. 老家	（名）	lǎojiā	native place
4. 农村	（名）	nóngcūn	countryside, rural area
5. 钓	（动）	diào	to fish
6. 顾	（动）	gù	to attend to, to take into consideration
7. 闻	（动）	wén	to smell
8. 股	（量）	gǔ	(a measure word)
9. 臭	（形）	chòu	foul, stinking
10. 污水	（名）	wūshuǐ	foul water, polluted water
11. 流动	（动）	liúdòng	to flow
12. 别说…… 就连…… 也／都……		biéshuō… jiù lián… yě/dōu…	not to mention...even...
13. 虾	（名）	xiā	shrimp
14. 青蛙	（名）	qīngwā	frog
15. 乡亲	（名）	xiāngqīn	fellow villager or townsman
16. 上游	（名）	shàngyóu	upper reaches
17. 废	（形）	fèi	waste, useless
18. 工业	（名）	gōngyè	industry

19. 收入	（名）	shōurù	income
20. 落后	（动）	luòhòu	to fall behind
21. 减产	（动）	jiǎnchǎn	to drop in production
22. 县城	（名）	xiànchéng	county town
23. 上任	（动）	shàngrèn	to assume office
24. 县长	（名）	xiànzhǎng	county magistrate
25. 计	（名）	jì	stratagem
26. 眼前	（名）	yǎnqián	at present
27. 利益	（名）	lìyì	benefit, profit, interest
28. 长远	（形）	chángyuǎn	long-term, long-range
29. 彻底	（形）	chèdǐ	thorough
30. 治理	（动）	zhìlǐ	to harness, to regulate
31. 宁可……也……		nìngkě…yě…	would rather...than (not)...
32. 告别	（动）	gàobié	to part from, to say goodbye to
33. 现实	（名）	xiànshí	reality

补充词汇　Supplementary words

1. 下游	（名）	xiàyóu	lower reaches
2. 寒假	（名）	hánjià	winter vacation
3. 提供	（动）	tígōng	to offer, to provide, to supply
4. 仅仅	（副）	jǐnjǐn	only, barely, simply
5. 平衡	（动、形）	pínghéng	to balance; balanced
6. 迅速	（形）	xùnsù	rapid, swift, speedy
7. 人类	（名）	rénlèi	humanity, mankind
8. 空间	（名）	kōngjiān	space
9. 论证	（动）	lùnzhèng	to expound and prove
10. 森林	（名）	sēnlín	forest
11. 威胁	（动）	wēixié	to threaten
12. 经费	（名）	jīngfèi	outlay
13. 危机	（名）	wēijī	crisis

三 课堂练习 Exercises

（一）语音

1. 辨音辨调

shǔjià	暑假	liúshuǐ	流水	shàngyóu	上游
shūjià	书架	wūshuǐ	污水	xiàyóu	下游
gōngyuē	公约	shànrèn	善任	zhìlǐ	治理
gōngyè	工业	shàngrèn	上任	shìlǐ	事理

2. 朗读古诗

静夜思

[唐]李白

床前明月光，疑是地上霜。

举头望明月，低头思故乡。

回乡偶书

[唐]贺知章

少小离家老大回，乡音无改鬓毛衰。

儿童相见不相识，笑问客从何处来。

（二）词语

从本课生词表中选择合适的词语填空

（1）快到________了，今年________我和全家人准备去山上滑雪。

（2）你________，这是什么味儿？

（3）一下雨，这里到处是污水，可________了。

（4）这条河的________有好几个工厂，污染了河水，________的老百姓连喝水都有了困难。

(5) 这个国家以前很乱，现在________得真不错。

(6) 王欢回到________，________们都来看他。

(7) 我们的院长刚刚________，他还不太了解情况。

(8) 一日之________在于晨，一年之________在于春。

(9) 小田的老家在________，不在城市。

(10) 我们要互相关心、互相照顾，不能只________自己的________，不________别人的________。

(11) 这里是中国最大的________区。

(12) 你找的人远在天边，近在________。

(13) 经过努力，他们的理想变成了________。

(14) 回国以前，我跟老师和同学们________。

(15) 学校为同学们的生活和学习________了很多方便的条件。

(16) 为了把问题搞清楚，必须做________的调查。

(17) 他________用了半个钟头就做完了试验。

(18) 保护环境，努力________人类和大自然之间的关系，每个人都有责任。

(19) 那些孩子很聪明，________明白老师的意思。

(20) 由于改革开放，这个国家的经济得到________的发展。

(21) 不能只顾眼前，你有没有一个________计划？

(22) 地球是人类生活的________。

(23) 经过________，这个计划半年就能实现。

(24) 这个地区还没开发，大________里有许多珍贵的动物。

(25) 这个地区经济的发展不________，有的地方比较先进，有的地方比较落后。

(26) 这个县的工业发展很快，可是农业还比较________。

(27) 环境污染________着人类的生存。

(28) 这次去桂林，公司为职员提供了旅游的________。

（三）句型

1. 替换

（1）咱们俩明天或者去逛公园，或者去爬山，你定吧！

去逛公园	去看球赛
去爬山	进城
进城买东西	去农村看看
去钓鱼	去游泳
去滑冰	去看冰灯
去访问	去参观
参观学校	参观幼儿园
看电影	去茶馆儿
去图书馆看书	去教室学习
去看展览	去看京剧

（2）我明天不是去逛公园，就是去爬山。

去逛公园	去看球赛
去爬山	进城
进城买东西	去农村看看
去钓鱼	去游泳
去滑冰	去看冰灯
去访问	去参观
参观学校	参观幼儿园
看电影	去茶馆儿
去图书馆看书	去教室学习
去看展览	去看京剧

（3）他宁可饿肚子，也不吃剩饭。

吃不饱	不偷东西
骑自行车	不坐汽车
多花钱	不丢面子

挨骂	不说
挨打	不说
不吃饭	要去看冰灯
不去看球赛	要给我辅导
不休息	要帮助别人
不上课	要陪我去医院
不买水果	要买书

（4）河里别说鱼虾了，就连青蛙也见不到一只了。

这个问题	是我	学习最好的同学	回答不了
这个问题	孩子	大人	说不清
那顿饭	酒	肉	没有
那里	树	草	不长
那儿	是大路	小路	没有
我这儿	钢笔	铅笔	没有
我	打网球	打乒乓球	不会
他	是肉	鸡蛋	不吃
他	处长	科长	不是
今年	水果	青菜	很少

（5）河里连青蛙也见不到一只了，何况鱼虾呢？

这个问题	学习最好的同学	回答不了	我
这个问题	大人	说不清	孩子
那顿饭	肉	没有	酒
那里	草	不长	树
那儿	小路	没有	大路
我这儿	铅笔	没有	钢笔
我	打乒乓球	不会	打网球
他	鸡蛋	不吃	肉
他	科长	不是	处长
今年	青菜	很少	水果

2. 选词填空

还　　再　　更　　并且　　特别是

(1) 丁兰会跳舞，________能教跳舞。

(2) 我喜欢动物，________喜欢熊猫。

(3) 彼得已经去过三次长城了，他想今年暑假________去一次。

(4) 艾米除了学习汉语，________学习日语。

(5) 贝拉喜欢打球，________喜欢打太极拳。

(6) 汉语很难，________汉字。

(7) 我们班的同学都参加了汉语水平考试，________取得了很好的成绩。

(8) 我已经学了汉语、日语，明年开始________学一门韩国语。

(9) 我们在北京游览了长城、故宫，________吃了烤鸭、看了京剧。

(10) 我喜欢夏天，________喜欢秋天，因为秋天是收获的季节。

四 家庭作业 Homework

(一) 阅读

保护环境

据有关专家论证，在遥远的古代，5万年前的地球上约有几十万人，一万年前约有500万人。那时候，地球上三分之二的面积是森林，生活环境十分优美。

随着社会文明的发展，人口一年比一年多。1830年世界上人口为10亿，1974年就增加到40亿，到1987年已经达到50亿。现在世界上每小时就大约有15000个婴儿出生，也就是说，每天地球上就要多出30多万人。地球不会变大，而居住在地球上的人却迅速增加，这个世界变得越来越拥挤，加上人类不注意保护地球环境，人类的生存因此受到极大的威胁。

人要生存，要发展，就要有一定的空间，有的国家每平方公里居住的人口已达到260人。这样下去，再过几百年，世界不知会变成什么样子。

人类对环境的破坏也使人类和大自然的关系越来越不平衡。人要吃饭，要喝水，要有房子住，可是，大自然是不是还能提供足够的粮食、水和建筑材料呢？当然，科学的发展和技术的进步能给人们提供更好的生活环境，提高人类的健康水平，但是，科学技术的进步仅仅给人类提供了发展的条件，不能彻底解决环境问题带来的危机。

世界是一个大家庭，生活在地球上的每个人，对世界的未来都有责任。为了人类的未来，我们必须注意保护环境，珍爱人类的母亲——地球。

1. 连线

环境	水平
保护	文明
社会	优美
迅速	解决
建筑	环境
健康	增加
完全	材料

2. 根据上下文猜下列词语的意思

（1）遥远——

（2）婴儿——

（3）居住——

（4）生存——

（5）因此——

（6）足够——

（7）珍爱——

3. 讨论题

（1）在遥远的古代，地球上的情况是怎么样的？

（2）随着社会文明的发展，地球环境发生了什么变化？

（3）人类为什么要保护环境？

（二）词语

1. 用下列生词至少组成两个短语

（1）故乡：________ ________　　（2）落后：________ ________

（3）告别：________ ________　　（4）提供：________ ________

（5）保护：________ ________　　（6）治理：________ ________

（7）彻底：________ ________　　（8）迅速：________ ________

2. 用下列词语完成句子

顾

（1）大家都不喜欢那个年轻人，他只________，不________。

（2）老张要求自己很严格，他一生都是只________，不________。

（3）我们要为子孙后代造福，不能只________，不________。

（4）昨天下午我只________，忘了去开会。

（5）这么多事情，你一个人________吗？

（6）小陈________，从火里救出一个孩子。

宁　可

（1）我________，也要把这些事情做完。

（2）他们________，也不污染环境。

（3）艾米________，也不跟贝拉一起来。

（4）母亲________，也要给孩子买那件生日礼物。

(1) 你别送了，咱们就在这儿________。

(2) 王欢________，又回到北京。

(3) 你怎么没________？

(4) 我跟________的时候，她哭了。

(5) 我没想到那么多人来________。

(三) 句型

完成句子

(1) 我不但会唱歌，____________________。

(2) 他不但是我们的朋友，____________________。

(3) 他不但会说汉语，____________________。

(4) 贝拉不但喜欢游泳，____________________。

(5) 王才不但努力学习，____________________。

(6) 我们不但看得清楚，____________________。

(7) 这个练习很难，不但学生不会做，____________________。

(8) 不但年轻人喜欢这个运动，____________________。

(9) 不但小孩子喜欢熊猫，____________________。

(10) 不但妻子做家务活儿，____________________。

(11) 这里的环境不错，不但学习环境很好，____________________。

(12) 这个地区污染很严重，不但河水污染了，____________________。

(四) 写作

请写一写《我的故乡》，不少于500字。

五 语法 Grammar

（一）选择复句　Alternative complex sentences

分句之间具有选择关系的复句叫选择复句。这种复句可分为两小类：

Complex sentences in which there is an alternative relation between the clauses are known as alternative complex sentences. This kind of complex sentences can be divided into two categories.

1. 表示任选，例如“（还）是……还是……”“或者……或者……”“不是……就是……”等。

One indicates optional choices, such as “(还)是……还是……” “或者……或者……” “不是……就是……”, etc.

“（还）是……还是……”与“或者……或者……”强调任一选择均有可能。“（还）是……还是……”用于疑问句，“或者……或者……”用于陈述句。例如：

“(还)是……还是……” and “或者……或者……” stress on the possibility of either choice. “(还)是……还是……” is used in questions, “或者……或者……” is used in declarative sentences. E.g.:

（1）你是喜欢看京剧（呢），还是喜欢看话剧（呢）？

（2）我明天或者去逛公园，或者去爬山，或者去电影院，反正不在家休息。

（3）我每个星期天都不在学校，或者去逛公园，或者去爬山，或者去电影院。

“不是……就是……”强调二者只居其一，不能兼而有之。“不是”之前可加假设连词“如果”等。例如：

“不是……就是……” emphasizes the possibility of either-or choice. The hypothetical conjunction “如果” and so on can be placed before “不是”. E.g.:

（4）今天不是你请客，就是他请客。

（5）打起来，不是他伤了你，就是你伤了他。

2. 表示偏选，例如“宁可……也（不）……”。可以先说选取项，后说舍弃项；也可以先说舍弃项，后说选取项。例如：

Another indicates a preferable choice, such as “宁可……也(不)……”. The preferable choice can be preceded, as well as the discarded choice. E.g.:

（1）我宁可饿肚子，也不吃剩饭。

（2）宁可把河边的工厂都关了，也要为子孙后代留下一条清水河。

（二）递进复句 Progressive complex sentences

分句之间具有递进关系的复句叫递进复句。这种复句可分为三小类：

Complex sentences in which there is a progressive relation between the clauses are known as progressive complex sentences. This kind of complex sentences can be divided into three categories.

1. 顺进，表示由浅入深。其格式有“（不但／不仅）……，而且／并且／还／又／也……”“……，更……”“不但／不仅……，（而且）连……也／都……”“连……也／都（不／没）……，（更）别说／不用说……”“别说／不用说……，就是／就连……也／都……”等。例如：

One indicates a smooth progression, from the easy to the difficult and the complicated. The constructions are as follows: “(不但/不仅)……，而且/并且/还/又/也……” “……, 更……” “不但/不仅……, (而且)连……也/都……” “连……也/都(不/没)……, (更)别说/不用说……” “别说/不用说……, 就是/就连……也/都……”, etc. E.g.:

（1）他不但会唱歌，而且还会跳舞。

（2）他会唱歌，并且还会跳舞。

（3）他除了会唱歌，还会跳舞呢。

（4）他会唱歌，更会跳舞。

（5）他不但会唱歌，而且连跳舞都会。

（6）他连唱歌都不会，更不用说跳舞了。

（7）别说是唱歌了，就是跳舞，他也会。

2. 反进，表示从深到浅。其格式有“不但／不仅不／没……，而且还……”“不但／不仅不／没……，连……也／都不／没……”“别说／不用说……，连……也／都不／没……”等。例如：

Another indicates a contrary progression, from the complicated and the difficult to the easy. The constructions are as follows: “不但/不仅/没……, 而且还……” “不但/不仅不/没……, 连……也/都不/没……” “别说/不用说……, 连……也/都不/没……”, etc. E.g.:

（1）他不但不会跳舞，连唱歌都不会。

（2）别说是跳舞了，他连唱歌都不会。

3. 诘进，表示由浅入深或从深到浅。其格式有“……还（不／没）……，何况……”“连……也／都（不／没）……，何况……”等。例如：

The third indicates an interrogative progression, which can be from the easy to the difficult and the complicated, or from the complicated and the difficult to the easy. The constructions are as follows: “……还(不/没)……, 何况……” “连……也/都(不/没)……, 何况……,” etc. E.g.:

（1）他科长还没当上呢，何况处长呢？

（2）那座山连小树都没有，何况大树呢？

（3）这个会很重要，校长都参加了，何况一般干部呢？

（4）动画片《聪明的一休》连大人都喜欢看，何况孩子呢？

Dì-shí kè
第十课

参加中国人的婚礼

一 课文 Text

一天晚上，赵林给彼得送来了请柬，邀请彼得参加弟弟赵海的婚礼，彼得高兴地接受了邀请。

婚礼这天，彼得上午10点来到赵海举行婚礼的宾馆。最先迎接他的是宾馆大门上的红“囍”字。两个“喜”字靠在一起，还念“喜”吗？他正想着，赵林出来了，把他请进大厅里。彼得刚坐下，一个小伙子和一位姑娘迎了上来。小伙子身穿笔挺的西装，姑娘穿着白色的婚纱，头上戴着一朵红花。不用说，这就是新郎新娘了。赵林为他们做了介绍，彼得连忙送上他带来的礼物——一束鲜花。新郎新娘表示感谢，随后送了他一包喜糖。

大概因为彼得是“老外”的原因吧，他受到了特殊的招待。新郎陪他聊了好半天，还给他看了新房的照片。房间虽然不大，可是收拾得又整齐又漂亮。一套新家具，还有电视机、冰箱等，新房布置得既大方又典雅。

结婚典礼11点正式开始了。首先新郎新娘向父母鞠躬，接着向来宾们鞠躬，然后是夫妻互相鞠躬。在掌声和笑声中，主持人请这对新人讲述他们的恋爱经过，还让他俩唱了一支歌。歌声一停，有个小伙子就拿着一个用红线吊着的苹果走上来，让新郎新娘同时咬这个苹果，两个人咬了半天也没咬住……

最后，赵海单位的领导讲了话。她代表单位的全体职工向新郎新娘表示了热烈的祝贺，祝他们幸福美满、白头到老。她说："结婚是新生活的开始，希望你们互敬互爱，共度美好人生。另外，别忘了早生贵子哟。"这句话逗得大家哈哈大笑。

结婚典礼一结束，宴会紧接着就开始了。来宾们纷纷举起酒杯，祝福这对新人。

二 生词 New words

1. 请柬	（名）	qǐngjiǎn	invitation
2. 迎接	（动）	yíngjiē	to greet
3. 靠	（动）	kào	to lean against, to depend on
4. 笔挺	（形）	bǐtǐng	well-ironed
5. 西装	（名）	xīzhuāng	business suit
6. 婚纱	（名）	hūnshā	wedding gown
7. 随后	（副）	suíhòu	soon afterwards
8. 老外	（名）	lǎowài	foreigner
9. 特殊	（形）	tèshū	special
10. 家具	（名）	jiājù	furniture
11. 布置	（动）	bùzhì	to decorate, to arrange
12. 大方	（形）	dàfang	natural and poised
13. 典雅	（形）	diǎnyǎ	elegant

14. 正式	（形）	zhèngshì	formal
15. 来宾	（名）	láibīn	guest
16. 吊	（动）	diào	to hang
17. 咬	（动）	yǎo	to bite
18. 互敬互爱		hùjìng-hù'ài	to mutually respect and love
敬爱	（动）	jìng'ài	to respect and love
19. 早生贵子		zǎo shēng guìzǐ	may you have a baby soon
20. 纷纷	（副）	fēnfēn	one after another

补充词汇 Supplementary words

1. 理发	（动）	lǐfà	to have a haircut
2. 姻缘	（名）	yīnyuán	marriage
3. 恩爱	（形）	ēn'ài	affectionate
4. 总理	（名）	zǒnglǐ	premier, prime minister
5. 仪式	（名）	yíshì	ceremony
6. 会谈	（动）	huìtán	to talk
7. 讨好	（动）	tǎohǎo	to curry favor with, to play up to
8. 腐败	（形、动）	fǔbài	decayed; to corrupt
9. 瞎	（动、副）	xiā	to be blind; aimlessly, groundlessly
10. 座谈	（动）	zuòtán	to have an informal discussion
11. 报告	（动、名）	bàogào	to report; report
12. 签订	（动）	qiāndìng	to sign
13. 总结	（动、名）	zǒngjié	to sum up, to summarize; summary
14. 学期	（名）	xuéqī	term, semester
15. 会见	（动）	huìjiàn	to meet with
16. 迎亲	（动）	yíngqīn	to go to the bride's home to escort her back to the wedding
17. 稍微	（副）	shāowēi	slightly, a bit
18. 特定	（形）	tèdìng	specific
19. 告白	（动）	gàobái	to confess
20. 宣誓	（动）	xuānshì	to make an oath
21. 贺礼	（名）	hèlǐ	gift (as a token of congratulation)
22. 恭喜	（动）	gōngxǐ	to congratulate

23. 原封不动		yuánfēng bú dòng	to keep something wholly intact
24. 西式	（形）	xīshì	western style
中式	（形）	zhōngshì	Chinese style
25. 致敬	（动）	zhìjìng	to pay tribute to

专名　Proper nouns

1. 赵海	Zhào Hǎo	name of a person
2. 周礼	Zhōulǐ	The Rites of Zhou

二 课堂练习 Exercises

（一）语音

1. 辨音辨调

yīnjié	音节	yīnxiǎng	音响	zhèngshì	正式
yíngjiē	迎接	yǐngxiǎng	影响	zhòngshì	重视
sùcài	素菜	lǐfà	理发	dǎting	打听
shūcài	蔬菜	lìfǎ	立法	dàtīng	大厅

2. 读下面的俗语

（1）男大当婚，女大当嫁。

（2）室雅何须大，花香不在多。

（3）千里送鹅毛，礼轻情义重。

（4）千里姻缘一线牵，夫妻恩爱到白头。

（二）词语

从本课生词表中选择合适的词语填空

（1）我去机场________一个美国艺术代表团。

（2）你的房间________得真不错。

（3）他的生活习惯很________，跟别人都不一样。

（4）山本非常________，跟朋友出去总是他花钱。

（5）这个建筑又________又________。

（6）大内________在沙发上睡着了。

（7）赵林________自己的努力当上了工程师。

（8）中国总理首先举行欢迎仪式，________两国总理举行了________会谈。

（9）新郎身穿________的西装，新娘穿着白色________，他们照了一张相。

（10）别干那种费力不________的事儿。

（11）那个小伙子很会________领导，别人都看不起他。

（12）晚会结束了，同学们________走出礼堂。

（13）天气太热，他们带的食品都________了。

（14）政府要坚持反对________。

（15）那个老人的右眼________了。

（16）说话得有证据，不能________说。

（17）我的头发太长了，该________了。

（18）上学期我们开了两次________会，讨论学习方法问题。

（19）总理正在做政府工作________。

（20）我们________的孙校长退休了。

（21）这次贸易________非常成功，一共________了10项合作项目。

（22）校长先________了上学期的工作，紧接着又________了本学期的工作。

（23）客人们祝新郎新娘的美好________天长地久。

（三）句型

1. 替换

（1）新郎新娘 表示感谢，随后送了他一包喜糖。

他们	穿上西装	准备迎接客人
他们	举行了结婚典礼	一起去饭店吃饭
他们	一起照了相	一起去买家具
他们	买了家具	去买电视机
总理	会见了美国客人	和他们进行了友好的会谈
总理	举行了欢迎仪式	跟客人进行了会谈
校长	总结了上学期的工作	布置了下学期的工作
他	买了冰箱	又买了一台电视机
他	理了发	去买东西
他	买了蔬菜	又去买肉
他	去听报告	参加了座谈

（2）新郎新娘首先向父母鞠躬，接着向来宾们鞠躬。

他们	穿上西装	准备迎接客人
他们	举行了结婚典礼	一起去饭店吃饭
他们	一起照了相	一起去买家具
他们	买了家具	去买电视机
总理	会见了美国客人	和他们进行了友好的会谈
总理	举行了欢迎仪式	跟客人进行了会谈
校长	总结了上学期的工作	布置了下学期的工作
他	买了冰箱	又买了一台电视机
他	理了发	去买东西
他	买了蔬菜	又去买肉
他	去听报告	参加了座谈

2. 用“以后”“后来”“接着”“随后”“又”“再”填空

（1）他是前年调到我校来的，________走了。

（2）你回国________，有空儿给我来封信。

（3）我明天去故宫，后天________去颐和园。

（4）他做完作业________，又看了一会儿电视。

（5）我发完言了，你________发言吧。

（6）开始我和安娜在一个班，________她去外交学院了。

（7）他昨天进了一趟城，今天________进了一趟城。

（8）你别急，这件事儿我________再告诉你。

（9）你先走，我________就到。

（四）成段表达

用第一人称复述课文。

（五）功能会话：听后模仿

1. 猜测

（1）A：大内今天没去上课。

B：她可能病了。

（2）A：山本不想参加足球赛。

B：大概他身体不太好。

（3）A：他知道这件事儿吗？

B：也许不知道。

（4）A：他打算做什么工作？

B：他一定是去公司当翻译。

2. 埋怨

（1）A：奶奶，您老是想着攒钱。

B：不攒钱，以后拿什么给你娶媳妇？

（2）A：你的自行车我给骑坏了。

B：你这是怎么搞的！

3. 惊讶

（1）A：用不了多少，有个千儿八百的就够了。

B：我的天！一顿饭花那么多钱？

（2）A：不太贵，两千多块。

B：我的天！一套衣服花那么多钱？

4. 夸张

（1）A：你累不累？

B：我累得要命。

（2）A：他着急吗？

B：他急得心里直冒火。

（3）A：公园里的花儿怎么样？

B：公园里的花儿漂亮极了。

（4）A：你怎么了？

B：今天我倒霉透了！刚出家门，自行车就坏了。

（5）A：你这次考试怎么样？

B：这次考试糟糕透了，我有两道题没回答出来。

（6）A：我昨天感冒了，吃了五片药都没出汗，看来这挤车比吃药还灵。

B：以后你感冒别去医院了。

（7）A：哎，别挤了！再挤就成相片儿了。

B：看你说的。

5. 比喻

（1）A：你看，他高兴得跟孩子一样。

B：是啊，他怎么那么高兴？

（2）A：白老师，您家里书真多，跟个小图书馆一样。

B：你想看哪本，随便挑。

（3）A：艾米的爸爸是个书迷。

B：他看见好书就跟看见美酒一样。

（4）A：车里真挤。

B：可不是，跟沙丁鱼罐头似的，一点儿空隙也没有。

6. 催促

（1）A：几点了？

B：差10分钟9点，快走吧，不然就迟到了。

（2）A：你得赶快去，不然来不及了。

B：不着急，还有半个钟头呢。

（3）A：时间不多了，你得赶紧准备。

B：好吧。

（4）A：早点儿动身吧，别误了火车。

B：我马上就走。

（5）A：都什么时候了？还不走？

B：着什么急？我打车去，来得及！

四 家庭作业 Homework

（一）阅读

中国的婚礼

中国的婚礼主要是根据周礼来的，虽然各地民俗有所不同，但是迎亲、典礼、宴会等都基本保留了下来。

迎亲，参考的是古代迎亲<u>花轿</u>，多以租婚车来代替。中国是一个爱面子的国家，婚礼是人生大事，只要经济条件稍微好一点儿的家庭都会把婚礼办得很隆重。就上海来说，租一辆好的婚车最少需要3000元左右，一般车队有6辆或者8辆就可以了，花费大概在2万元左右。

典礼是婚礼的重要部分，对新郎新娘和来宾而言，婚礼是神圣的，每个环节都有着特定的仪式感。婚庆公司会推荐一名专业的婚礼司仪来主持婚礼。首先是婚礼的开场仪式，司仪负责说婚礼的开场白，引出新郎新娘的入场。新郎一般会从新娘父亲手中接过新娘的手，这是新娘父亲对新郎的一种责任传递。然后新郎新娘站在中间，在司仪的引导下说出爱情的告白和婚姻的宣誓，完成交换戒指等仪式。仪式结束后，新郎新娘就可以向来宾们敬酒了。

参加婚礼宴会的来宾都要给新郎新娘准备贺礼，恭喜新人。新郎新娘也会用喜糖等回礼。婚礼还会有不少喜糖是原封不动的，那些是用来送来不了的亲友们的。

虽然在中国的婚礼中有了一些西式婚礼的影子，例如新娘穿白色的婚纱等，但是中式婚礼已越来越多地吸引了年轻人。一场中式婚礼，既是对爱情的记录，又是对中国传统文化的致敬。

1. 根据上下文猜下列词语的意思

花轿——

推荐——

司仪——

开场白——

回礼——

2. 回答问题

（1）中国的婚礼中有哪些民俗是保留到现在的？

（2）婚礼中的重要部分是什么？

（3）中国的婚礼中有哪些西式婚礼的影子？与你们国家的婚礼有什么不同？

（二）词语

用下列生词至少组成两个短语

（1）迎接：________ ________

（2）布置：________ ________

（3）讨好：________ ________

（4）报告：________ ________

（5）特殊：________ ________

（6）大方：________ ________

（7）正式：________ ________

（8）纷纷：________ ________

（9）腐败：________ ________

（10）理发：________ ________

（11）靠：________ ________

（12）总结：________ ________

（三）写作

请写一写你们国家的婚礼，不少于500字。

五 语法 Grammar

承接复句 Successive complex sentences

分句之间具有先后相继关系的复句，称为承接复句。这种复句主要有以下几种格式：“……，接着／以后／后来／然后／随后……” “先／首先……，其次……” “（一）……，就／便……” “……，才／再／又……” 。例如：

Complex sentences in which there is a successive relation between the clauses are known as successive complex sentences. This kind of sentences are mainly as follows: “……, 接着/以后/后来/然后/随后……” “先/首先……, 其次……” “(一)……, 就/便……” “……, 才/再/又……”. E.g.:

（1）他写完了第一封信，接着写第二封信。

（2）他现在在初级班学习，以后去中级班学习。

（3）他当过两年售票员，后来又当了两年工人。

（4）他先学习英语，然后再学习法语。

（5）新郎新娘表示感谢，随后送了他一包喜糖。

（6）首先新郎新娘向父母鞠躬，接着向来宾们鞠躬，然后是夫妻互相鞠躬。

（7）学习首先要努力，其次要讲究方法。

（8）他一走出楼门口，就遇见了金汉成。

（9）他参观了学校，又参观了幼儿园。

（10）你从这儿往前走100米，再向右拐。

Glossary (Volume 7)
词汇总表（第7册）

A			
挨	（动）	āi	8
挨	（动）	ái	6
癌（症）	（名）	ái(zhèng)	4
唉	（叹）	ài	3
安装	（动）	ānzhuāng	2
B			
百货	（名）	bǎihuò	8
摆	（动）	bǎi	5
半夜	（名）	bànyè	2
报告	（动、名）	bàogào	10
报考	（动）	bàokǎo	3
悲痛	（形）	bēitòng	7
备注	（名）	bèizhù	1
背后	（名）	bèihòu	2
本	（副）	běn	8
本科	（名）	běnkē	3
本来	（副）	běnlái	8
笔挺	（形）	bǐtǐng	10
变质	（动）	biànzhì	4
便	（副）	biàn	1
标签	（名）	biāoqiān	8
表现	（动）	biǎoxiàn	3
别说……就 连……也／ 都……		biéshuō…jiù lián…yě/dōu …	9
宾至如归		bīnzhì-rúguī	8
冰箱	（名）	bīngxiāng	4
不料	（连）	búliào	4
不然	（连）	bùrán	6
布置	（动）	bùzhì	10
步	（名）	bù	3
C			
才能	（名）	cáinéng	3
材料	（名）	cáiliào	5
踩	（动）	cǎi	6
层次	（名）	céngcì	3
叉儿	（名）	chār	1
插	（动）	chā	1
产量	（名）	chǎnliàng	2
长处	（名）	chángchù	3
长远	（形）	chángyuǎn	9
畅销	（动）	chàngxiāo	8
彻底	（形）	chèdǐ	9
沉重	（形）	chénzhòng	6
成果	（名）	chéngguǒ	4
诚实	（形）	chéngshí	7
吃力	（形）	chīlì	6
冲	（动）	chōng	2
重复	（动）	chóngfù	2
臭	（形）	chòu	9
出路	（名）	chūlù	3
出谋划策		chūmóu- huàcè	8
初级	（形）	chūjí	1
处理	（动）	chǔlǐ	2
创建	（动）	chuàngjiàn	7
瓷	（名）	cí	5

从事	（动）	cóngshì	1
促使	（动）	cùshǐ	3
D			
打工	（动）	dǎgōng	7
打折	（动）	dǎzhé	8
大吃大喝		dàchī-dàhē	5
大胆	（形）	dàdǎn	3
大方	（形）	dàfang	10
担心	（动）	dānxīn	4
当……时		dāng…shí	6
当初	（名）	dāngchū	8
当今	（名）	dāngjīn	5
到……为止		dào…wéizhǐ	8
倒	（动）	dào	5
倒数	（动）	dàoshǔ	6
典礼	（名）	diǎnlǐ	5
典雅	（形）	diǎnyǎ	10
电梯	（名）	diàntī	6
吊	（动）	diào	10
钓	（动）	diào	9
调查	（动）	diàochá	1
订婚	（动）	dìnghūn	1
豆（子）	（名）	dòu(zi)	4
逗	（动）	dòu	1
独	（副）	dú	3
独资	（形）	dúzī	3
肚皮	（名）	dùpí	6
对策	（名）	duìcè	6
对话	（动）	duìhuà	4
多彩	（形）	duōcǎi	4
多么	（副）	duōme	4
多数	（名）	duōshù	8

E			
恩爱	（形）	ēn'ài	10
F			
发明	（动、名）	fāmíng	6
法官	（名）	fǎguān	4
繁荣	（形）	fánróng	8
反而	（副）	fǎn'ér	6
反复	（副）	fǎnfù	7
返	（动）	fǎn	3
……犯		…fàn	5
放弃	（动）	fàngqì	3
废	（形）	fèi	9
费	（动）	fèi	6
分析	（动）	fēnxī	2
纷纷	（副）	fēnfēn	10
粉碎	（形）	fěnsuì	5
奋斗	（动）	fèndòu	7
丰盛	（形）	fēngshèng	5
封面	（名）	fēngmiàn	1
奉献	（动）	fèngxiàn	2
夫人	（名）	fūrén	6
服装	（名）	fúzhuāng	8
腐败	（形、动）	fǔbài	10
妇女	（名）	fùnǚ	2
复杂	（形）	fùzá	1
富强	（形）	fùqiáng	7
G			
改革	（动）	gǎigé	8
干	（副）	gān	5
干脆	（副）	gāncuì	6
赶	（动）	gǎn	7
告白	（动）	gàobái	10

告别	（动）	gàobié	9
革新	（动）	géxīn	2
个体	（名）	gètǐ	8
根据	（介）	gēnjù	3
工业	（名）	gōngyè	9
工艺	（名）	gōngyì	8
工整	（形）	gōngzhěng	1
工资	（名）	gōngzī	2
公关	（名）	gōngguān	3
恭喜	（动）	gōngxǐ	10
钩儿	（名）	gōur	1
股	（量）	gǔ	9
鼓掌	（动）	gǔzhǎng	4
故乡	（名）	gùxiāng	9
顾	（动）	gù	9
顾客	（名）	gùkè	8
管理	（动）	guǎnlǐ	7
广告	（名）	guǎnggào	6
规模	（名）	guīmó	7
锅	（名）	guō	2
国籍	（名）	guójí	1
过分	（形）	guòfèn	3
过奖	（动）	guòjiǎng	1
H			
寒假	（名）	hánjià	9
合资	（动）	hézī	3
合作	（动）	hézuò	1
何况	（连）	hékuàng	3
贺礼	（名）	hèlǐ	10
喝彩	（动）	hècǎi	4
互敬互爱		hùjìng-hù'ài	10
花花绿绿	（形）	huāhuālǜlǜ	8
华侨	（名）	huáqiáo	7
话筒	（名）	huàtǒng	2
欢呼	（动）	huānhū	4
欢喜	（形）	huānxǐ	7
灰心	（形）	huīxīn	6
汇报	（动）	huìbào	4
会话	（动）	huìhuà	4
会见	（动）	huìjiàn	10
会谈	（动）	huìtán	10
婚否		hūn fǒu	1
婚礼	（名）	hūnlǐ	4
婚纱	（名）	hūnshā	10
获得	（动）	huòdé	4
J			
极其	（副）	jíqí	5
急救车	（名）	jíjiùchē	5
计	（名）	jì	9
记忆	（动）	jìyì	5
记者	（名）	jìzhě	5
技术员	（名）	jìshùyuán	5
继承	（动）	jìchéng	7
加班	（动）	jiābān	2
家具	（名）	jiājù	10
（家）宴	（名）	(jiā)yàn	7
假如	（连）	jiǎrú	4
价格	（名）	jiàgé	8
艰苦	（形）	jiānkǔ	7
检讨	（动）	jiǎntǎo	5
检讨书	（名）	jiǎntǎoshū	5
减产	（动）	jiǎnchǎn	9
简历	（名）	jiǎnlì	3
建设	（动）	jiànshè	1
鉴定	（动）	jiàndìng	2
将来	（名）	jiānglái	1
讲述	（动）	jiǎngshù	7
奖	（动、名）	jiǎng	1

骄傲	（形）	jiāo'ào	3
脚步	（名）	jiǎobù	8
教材	（名）	jiàocái	1
教堂	（名）	jiàotáng	4
皆	（副）	jiē	6
接待	（动）	jiēdài	2
接风	（动）	jiēfēng	7
仅仅	（副）	jǐnjǐn	9
尽管	（连）	jǐnguǎn	3
尽	（动）	jìn	7
劲儿	（名）	jìnr	4
经费	（名）	jīngfèi	9
经营	（动）	jīngyíng	8
精力	（名）	jīnglì	7
精细	（形）	jīngxì	8
精心	（形）	jīngxīn	8
景象	（名）	jǐngxiàng	8
竟	（副）	jìng	6
敬爱	（动）	jìng'ài	10
救星	（名）	jiùxīng	6
局长	（名）	júzhǎng	5
捐	（动）	juān	7
决	（副）	jué	4
决心	（名）	juéxīn	3
绝对	（副）	juéduì	8
K			
开发	（动）	kāifā	2
开放	（动）	kāifàng	8
靠	（动）	kào	10
可见	（连）	kějiàn	4
空	（形）	kōng	2
空间	（名）	kōngjiān	9
空头	（形）	kōngtóu	2
恐怕	（副）	kǒngpà	3
扣	（动）	kòu	6
扣眼儿	（名）	kòuyǎnr	6
苦恼	（形）	kǔnǎo	6
款式	（名）	kuǎnshì	8
L			
来宾	（名）	láibīn	10
栏目	（名）	lánmù	1
懒	（形）	lǎn	5
老家	（名）	lǎojiā	9
老外	（名）	lǎowài	10
理发	（动）	lǐfà	10
力	（名）	lì	5
立即	（副）	lìjí	6
利益	（名）	lìyì	9
凉	（形）	liáng	6
粮食	（名）	liángshi	2
了却	（动）	liǎoquè	7
临	（介）	lín	7
灵活	（形）	línghuó	7
铃声	（名）	língshēng	1
流动	（动）	liúdòng	9
隆重	（形）	lóngzhòng	7
楼梯	（名）	lóutī	6
旅馆	（名）	lǚguǎn	2
论证	（动）	lùnzhèng	9
落	（动）	luò	2
落后	（动）	luòhòu	9
M			
马虎	（形）	mǎhu	1
迈	（动）	mài	3
美德	（名）	měidé	7
美观	（形）	měiguān	8
门	（量）	mén	3

秘书	（名）	mìshū	2
面前	（名）	miànqián	5
面试	（动）	miànshì	3
面试官	（名）	miànshìguān	3
名单	（名）	míngdān	1
名贵	（形）	míngguì	8
模糊	（形）	móhu	8
模特儿	（名）	mótèr	8
默默	（副）	mòmò	2
母校	（名）	mǔxiào	7
		N	
哪怕……也／都……		nǎpà…yě/dōu…	6
难怪	（副）	nánguài	5
难受	（形）	nánshòu	5
能力	（名）	nénglì	3
宁可……也……		nìngkě…yě…	9
农村	（名）	nóngcūn	9
		O	
哦	（叹）	ó	2
哦	（叹）	ò	2
呕吐	（动）	ǒutù	5
		P	
拍	（动）	pāi	6
跑步	（动）	pǎobù	6
培训	（动）	péixùn	3
培养	（动）	péiyǎng	7
配偶	（名）	pèi'ǒu	1
皮带	（名）	pídài	6
平	（形）	píng	5
平安	（形）	píng'ān	4
平衡	（动、形）	pínghéng	9
评	（动）	píng	4
评选	（动）	píngxuǎn	4
凭	（介）	píng	7
		Q	
期限	（名）	qīxiàn	1
企业	（名）	qǐyè	3
气	（动）	qì	5
气候	（名）	qìhòu	4
恰恰	（副）	qiàqià	4
签订	（动）	qiāndìng	10
巧克力	（名）	qiǎokèlì	6
切	（动）	qiē	4
勤劳	（形）	qínláo	7
青年	（名）	qīngnián	5
青蛙	（名）	qīngwā	9
清白	（形）	qīngbái	5
请柬	（名）	qǐngjiǎn	10
求	（动）	qiú	3
求职	（动）	qiúzhí	3
全部	（形）	quánbù	7
确定	（形、动）	quèdìng	5
		R	
人才	（名）	réncái	3
人际	（形）	rénjì	3
人类	（名）	rénlèi	9
人员	（名）	rényuán	2
扔	（动）	rēng	2
荣获	（动）	rónghuò	4
荣誉	（名）	róngyù	4
入	（动）	rù	1
		S	
森林	（名）	sēnlín	9

商场	（名）	shāngchǎng	2
商品	（名）	shāngpǐn	3
商业	（名）	shāngyè	8
上任	（动）	shàngrèn	9
上游	（名）	shàngyóu	9
稍微	（副）	shāowēi	10
设	（动）	shè	7
设备	（名）	shèbèi	2
申请	（动）	shēnqǐng	1
深刻	（形）	shēnkè	5
甚至	（连）	shènzhì	3
胜利	（动）	shènglì	8
剩	（动）	shèng	4
失败	（动）	shībài	3
失去	（动）	shīqù	8
时装	（名）	shízhuāng	8
实习	（动）	shíxí	3
始终	（副）	shǐzhōng	7
事故	（名）	shìgù	4
事业	（名）	shìyè	7
试验	（动）	shìyàn	2
收获	（动、名）	shōuhuò	4
收入	（名）	shōurù	9
手续	（名）	shǒuxù	1
书记	（名）	shūjì	5
暑假	（名）	shǔjià	9
双方	（名）	shuāngfāng	2
睡眠	（名）	shuìmián	6
思念	（动）	sīniàn	7
送行	（动）	sòngxíng	7
速度	（名）	sùdù	2
算账	（动）	suànzhàng	2
随后	（副）	suíhòu	10
碎	（形）	suì	5
损失	（动、名）	sǔnshī	4

T			
摊位	（名）	tānwèi	8
讨好	（动）	tǎohǎo	10
特定	（形）	tèdìng	10
特殊	（形）	tèshū	10
提供	（动）	tígōng	9
体会	（动）	tǐhuì	5
挑剔	（动）	tiāoti	8
通过	（动）	tōngguò	2
通信	（动）	tōngxìn	1
头脑	（名）	tóunǎo	7
投	（形）	tóu	5
吐	（动）	tù	4
团聚	（动）	tuánjù	7
推销	（动）	tuīxiāo	3
退休	（动）	tuìxiū	7
拖	（动）	tuō	6
W			
哇	（助）	wa	2
外交	（名）	wàijiāo	1
外商	（名）	wàishāng	2
危机	（名）	wēijī	9
威胁	（动）	wēixié	9
未	（副）	wèi	1
未婚妻	（名）	wèihūnqī	1
未来	（形、名）	wèilái	1
文明	（形、名）	wénmíng	8
闻	（动）	wén	9
污染	（动）	wūrǎn	4
污水	（名）	wūshuǐ	9
无疑	（动）	wúyí	5
误解	（动、名）	wùjiě	3
悟	（动）	wù	5

X			
西式	（形）	xīshì	10
西装	（名）	xīzhuāng	10
吸引	（动）	xīyǐn	6
虾	（名）	xiā	9
瞎	（动、副）	xiā	10
下级	（名）	xiàjí	5
下游	（名）	xiàyóu	9
先进	（形）	xiānjìn	1
显著	（形）	xiǎnzhù	6
县城	（名）	xiànchéng	9
县长	（名）	xiànzhǎng	9
现实	（名）	xiànshí	9
限制	（动）	xiànzhì	6
线	（名）	xiàn	2
乡亲	（名）	xiāngqīn	9
相反	（形）	xiāngfǎn	4
详细	（形）	xiángxì	3
想念	（动）	xiǎngniàn	7
向往	（动）	xiàngwǎng	3
相声	（名）	xiàngsheng	4
项	（量）	xiàng	1
销毁	（动）	xiāohuǐ	5
小品	（名）	xiǎopǐn	4
校庆	（名）	xiàoqìng	7
心疼	（动）	xīnténg	6
心血	（名）	xīnxuè	4
心意	（名）	xīnyì	7
心愿	（名）	xīnyuàn	7
心脏	（名）	xīnzàng	6
新式	（形）	xīnshì	6
新颖	（形）	xīnyǐng	8
信仰	（名）	xìnyǎng	1
兴旺	（形）	xīngwàng	8
性别	（名）	xìngbié	1
宣布	（动）	xuānbù	2
宣誓	（动）	xuānshì	10
选	（动）	xuǎn	1
学期	（名）	xuéqī	10
学位	（名）	xuéwèi	7
询问	（动）	xúnwèn	8
迅速	（形）	xùnsù	9
Y			
眼前	（名）	yǎnqián	9
腰	（名）	yāo	6
咬	（动）	yǎo	10
也许	（副）	yěxǔ	8
业务	（名）	yèwù	2
一面…… 一面……		yímiàn… yímiàn…	6
宜		yí	6
仪式	（名）	yíshì	10
一方面…… 一方面……		yì fāngmiàn… yì fāngmiàn…	8
一针见血		yìzhēn-jiànxiě	5
议论	（动）	yìlùn	6
姻缘	（名）	yīnyuán	10
引进	（动）	yǐnjìn	2
迎	（动）	yíng	8
迎接	（动）	yíngjiē	10
迎亲	（动）	yíngqīn	10
影子	（名）	yǐngzi	6
勇敢	（形）	yǒnggǎn	7
用意	（名）	yòngyì	5
犹豫	（形）	yóuyù	8
有效	（形）	yǒuxiào	1
娱乐	（动、名）	yúlè	4

与其	（连）	yǔqí	3
原封不动		yuánfēng bú dòng	10
Z			
在乎	（动）	zàihu	2
早生贵子		zǎo shēng guìzǐ	10
则	（量）	zé	6
掌	（名）	zhǎng	4
掌声	（名）	zhǎngshēng	4
招聘	（动）	zhāopìn	3
招收	（动）	zhāoshōu	3
照例	（副）	zhàolì	6
……者		…zhě	3
整整	（副）	zhěngzhěng	5
正式	（形）	zhèngshì	10
证据	（名）	zhèngjù	5
政策	（名）	zhèngcè	6
症状	（名）	zhèngzhuàng	5
之	（助）	zhī	4
支持	（动）	zhīchí	2
支票	（名）	zhīpiào	2
肢	（名）	zhī	5
至少	（副）	zhìshǎo	5
至于	（介）	zhìyú	1
制定	（动）	zhìdìng	1
治理	（动）	zhìlǐ	9

致敬	（动）	zhìjìng	10
中级	（形）	zhōngjí	1
中式	（形）	zhōngshì	10
中	（动）	zhòng	4
中毒	（动）	zhòngdú	4
周年	（名）	zhōunián	7
粥	（名）	zhōu	6
主动	（形）	zhǔdòng	8
驻	（动）	zhù	1
专业	（名）	zhuānyè	1
桩	（量）	zhuāng	7
装模作样		zhuāngmú-zuòyàng	5
装作	（动）	zhuāngzuò	2
资本	（名）	zīběn	1
资金	（名）	zījīn	3
子孙	（名）	zǐsūn	7
自动	（形）	zìdòng	2
宗教	（名）	zōngjiào	1
总结	（动、名）	zǒngjié	10
总理	（名）	zǒnglǐ	10
祖国	（名）	zǔguó	2
最后	（名）	zuìhòu	3
左撇子	（名）	zuǒpiězi	4
座谈	（动）	zuòtán	10
做工	（名）	zuògōng	8

专名　Proper nouns

F		
冯明	Féng Míng	6
付	Fù	5
复康药店	Fùkāng Yàodiàn	6
H		
华	Huá	1
黄（帝）	Huáng(dì)	7
L		
李时珍	Lí Shízhēn	5
N		
牛思华	Niú Sīhuá	7
Q		
全聚德	Quánjùdé	7

T		
田	Tián	8
W		
万	Wàn	5
五粮液	Wǔliángyè	5
Y		
炎（帝）	Yán(dì)	7
Z		
赵海	Zhào Hǎo	10
周礼	Zhōulǐ	10

Glossary (Volume 1-Volume 6)
词汇总表（第1册—第6册）

A			
AA 制	（名）	AA zhì	6-1
阿		ā	4-7
阿姨	（名）	āyí	4-7
啊	（叹）	ā	2-6
啊	（叹）	à	3-5
啊	（助）	a	4-1
哎	（叹）	āi	4-1
哎呀	（叹）	āiyā	2-6
矮	（形）	ǎi	5-2
爱	（动）	ài	5-2
爱好	（名）	àihào	3-6
爱面子		ài miànzi	5-10
爱情	（名）	àiqíng	5-4
爱人	（名）	àiren	3-2
安静	（形）	ānjìng	5-3
安排	（动）	ānpái	6-1
安全	（形）	ānquán	4-9
安全带	（名）	ānquándài	6-2
安慰	（动）	ānwèi	5-8
按	（介）	àn	3-8
按时	（副）	ànshí	3-4
按照	（介）	ànzhào	3-8
澳元	（名）	àoyuán	6-10
B			
八	（数）	bā	1-1
把	（量）	bǎ	3-7
把	（介）	bǎ	4-8
爸爸	（名）	bàba	1-9
吧	（助）	ba	1-4
白	（形）	bái	1-9
白酒	（名）	báijiǔ	4-6
白天	（名）	báitiān	3-2
白头到老		báitóu-dàolǎo	3-10
百	（数）	bǎi	3-2
百科全书		bǎikē quánshū	6-6
班	（名）	bān	2-2
搬	（动）	bān	3-7
办	（动）	bàn	1-10
办法	（名）	bànfǎ	1-7
办公	（动）	bàngōng	2-1
办公室	（名）	bàngōngshì	3-8
办理	（动）	bànlǐ	6-9
半	（数）	bàn	2-8
半天	（数量）	bàntiān	2-10
帮	（动）	bāng	1-4
帮忙	（动）	bāngmáng	5-1
帮助	（动）	bāngzhù	1-8
棒	（形）	bàng	6-10
包	（动）	bāo	3-5
包裹	（名）	bāoguǒ	3-5
包装	（名、动）	bāozhuāng	3-5
包子	（名）	bāozi	6-1
薄	（形）	báo	6-9
饱	（形）	bǎo	5-3
宝贝	（名）	bǎobei	6-10
宝库	（名）	bǎokù	6-8
保存	（动）	bǎocún	5-3

保护	（动）	bǎohù	6-8
保龄球	（名）	bǎolíngqiú	4-5
保卫	（动）	bǎowèi	5-8
保卫处	（名）	bǎowèichù	5-8
保证	（动）	bǎozhèng	4-4
保证书	（名）	bǎozhèngshū	4-4
保质期	（名）	bǎozhìqī	5-3
报	（名）	bào	3-5
报名	（动）	bàomíng	4-1
报站	（动）	bàozhàn	5-6
报纸	（名）	bàozhǐ	4-10
抱	（动）	bào	4-8
抱歉	（形）	bàoqiàn	4-2
杯	（量）	bēi	3-6
杯子	（名）	bēizi	5-1
背	（动）	bēi	4-8
北	（名）	běi	3-1
北方	（名）	běifāng	3-5
北门	（名）	běimén	3-1
北面	（名）	běimiàn	4-2
背	（名）	bèi	5-8
倍	（量）	bèi	5-6
被	（介）	bèi	5-5
辈子	（名）	bèizi	5-7
奔	（动）	bēn	5-4
本	（量）	běn	2-2
本	（代）	běn	4-4
本子	（名）	běnzi	2-2
笨	（形）	bèn	5-10
鼻子	（名）	bízi	2-9
比	（动）	bǐ	3-1
比	（介）	bǐ	5-2
比价	（名）	bǐjià	3-8
比较	（副）	bǐjiào	1-10

比较	（动）	bǐjiào	4-5
比如	（动）	bǐrú	5-2
比赛	（动）	bǐsài	3-1
笔	（名）	bǐ	2-2
笔	（量）	bǐ	6-6
笔记本	（名）	bǐjìběn	3-10
笔记本电脑		bǐjìběn diànnǎo	3-10
笔试	（动）	bǐshì	1-10
必	（副）	bì	4-10
必须	（副）	bìxū	4-10
必需	（动）	bìxū	6-10
必需品	（名）	bìxūpǐn	6-10
毕竟	（副）	bìjìng	6-10
毕业	（动）	bìyè	4-4
碧螺春	（名）	bìluóchūn	6-7
扁	（形）	biǎn	6-1
变	（动）	biàn	5-2
变化	（名）	biànhuà	5-2
变迁	（动）	biànqiān	6-6
遍	（动、量）	biàn	4-3
表	（名）	biǎo	1-6
表示	（动）	biǎoshì	4-10
表演	（动）	biǎoyǎn	3-9
表扬	（动）	biǎoyáng	4-2
别	（副）	bié	1-6
别的	（代）	biéde	3-9
别人	（代）	biéren	2-9
宾馆	（名）	bīnguǎn	2-3
兵	（名）	bīng	4-3
兵马俑	（名）	bīngmǎyǒng	4-3
并	（副）	bìng	4-6
并	（连）	bìng	5-8
并且	（连）	bìngqiě	5-8
病	（动）	bìng	2-9

病房	（名）	bìngfáng	4-8
病人	（名）	bìngrén	4-10
拨打	（动）	bōdǎ	6-9
波浪	（名）	bōlàng	6-6
玻璃	（名）	bōli	3-3
播	（动）	bō	6-10
博士	（名）	bóshì	5-6
不错	（形）	búcuò	2-8
不但	（连）	búdàn	4-1
不断	（副）	búduàn	3-10
不对	（形）	búduì	2-1
不过	（连）	búguò	2-8
不见不散		bújiàn-búsàn	4-2
不愧	（副）	búkuì	6-5
不是……而是……		bú shì…ér shì…	6-3
不是……就是……		bú shì… jiù shì…	4-9
不用	（副）	búyòng	2-7
补	（动）	bǔ	6-10
补充	（动）	bǔchōng	6-7
不	（副）	bù	1-3
不得了	（形）	bùdéliǎo	4-8
不好意思		bù hǎoyìsi	3-7
不仅	（连）	bùjǐn	6-3
不巧		bù qiǎo	3-8
不如	（动）	bùrú	5-4
不同	（形）	bùtóng	6-1
部		bù	4-10
部	（量）	bù	6-6
部分	（名）	bùfen	3-5
部位	（名）	bùwèi	6-8
		C	
擦	（动）	cā	3-8
猜	（动）	cāi	2-1

才	（副）	cái	2-8
采	（动）	cǎi	6-3
彩色	（名）	cǎisè	6-4
菜	（名）	cài	1-4
菜	（名）	cài	2-8
菜单	（名）	càidān	4-6
菜地	（名）	càidì	2-8
菜名儿	（名）	càimíngr	4-5
参观	（动）	cānguān	4-3
参加	（动）	cānjiā	3-3
餐厅	（名）	cāntīng	3-6
残缺	（动）	cánquē	6-8
操场	（名）	cāochǎng	3-3
草	（名）	cǎo	4-10
草坪	（名）	cǎopíng	5-4
草原	（名）	cǎoyuán	5-8
册		cè	2-2
厕所	（名）	cèsuǒ	1-5
层	（量）	céng	2-3
曾	（副）	céng	4-3
曾经	（副）	céngjīng	4-3
茶	（名）	chá	2-9
茶馆儿	（名）	cháguǎnr	6-7
茶几	（名）	chájī	4-7
茶具	（名）	chájù	3-3
茶叶	（名）	cháyè	3-3
茶园	（名）	cháyuán	6-7
查	（动）	chá	3-7
差	（动）	chà	3-1
差不多	（副）	chàbuduō	4-5
产	（动）	chǎn	6-4
产品	（名）	chǎnpǐn	3-9
长	（形）	cháng	2-7
长度	（名）	chángdù	5-6

长期	（形）	chángqī	3-10
长寿	（形）	chángshòu	2-7
肠	（名）	cháng	4-10
肠胃炎	（名）	chángwèiyán	4-10
尝	（动）	cháng	2-9
常	（副）	cháng	1-6
场	（名、量）	chǎng	3-1
场所	（名）	chǎngsuǒ	6-7
唱歌	（动）	chànggē	2-7
超过	（动）	chāoguò	6-7
超市	（名）	chāoshì	1-6
超重	（动）	chāozhòng	3-5
朝	（介）	cháo	6-2
朝		cháo	6-3
朝代	（名）	cháodài	6-3
吵	（动）	chǎo	6-9
吵吵嚷嚷		chǎochǎorǎng-rǎng	6-9
吵嚷	（动）	chǎorǎng	6-9
炒	（动）	chǎo	4-6
车	（名）	chē	2-8
车窗	（名）	chēchuāng	6-2
车站	（名）	chēzhàn	3-3
沉	（动）	chén	6-7
衬衫	（名）	chènshān	3-9
称	（动）	chēng	6-6
称呼	（动）	chēnghu	6-5
称赞	（动）	chēngzàn	6-8
称作	（动）	chēngzuò	6-6
成	（动）	chéng	1-8
成功	（动）	chénggōng	4-4
成绩	（名）	chéngjì	3-2
成立	（动）	chénglì	6-8
成为	（动）	chéngwéi	5-5
诚信	（形）	chéngxìn	4-2

承认	（动）	chéngrèn	5-10
城	（名）	chéng	2-10
城市	（名）	chéngshì	2-10
吃	（动）	chī	1-4
吃苦	（动）	chīkǔ	5-7
迟到	（动）	chídào	3-7
充电器	（名）	chōngdiànqì	1-6
充分	（形）	chōngfèn	3-9
充满	（动）	chōngmǎn	5-6
重新	（副）	chóngxīn	3-5
抽	（动）	chōu	4-4
抽屉	（名）	chōuti	4-9
出	（动）	chū	2-4
出版	（动）	chūbǎn	3-6
出差	（动）	chūchāi	6-9
出发	（动）	chūfā	3-1
出口	（动）	chūkǒu	6-7
出生	（动）	chūshēng	2-6
出现	（动）	chūxiàn	6-8
出院	（动）	chūyuàn	4-10
出租	（动）	chūzū	2-8
出租车	（名）	chūzūchē	2-8
初		chū	5-7
除了……以外		chúle…yǐwài	3-10
厨房	（名）	chúfáng	4-7
处	（名）	chù	5-5
处长	（名）	chùzhǎng	6-9
穿	（动）	chuān	3-7
穿	（动）	chuān	5-6
穿越	（动）	chuānyuè	5-5
传	（动）	chuán	6-10
传说	（名）	chuánshuō	5-4
传统	（形）	chuántǒng	5-4
船	（名）	chuán	4-3

串	（量）	chuàn	6-8
窗户	（名）	chuānghu	3-8
床	（名）	chuáng	1-6
创造	（动）	chuàngzào	5-5
创作	（动）	chuàngzuò	6-8
吹	（动）	chuī	3-10
吹牛	（动）	chuīniú	4-8
春季	（名）	chūnjì	3-2
春天	（名）	chūntiān	3-2
词	（名）	cí	1-5
词典	（名）	cídiǎn	2-2
此	（代）	cǐ	5-9
次	（量）	cì	2-4
匆匆忙忙		cōngcōngmáng-máng	4-2
匆忙	（形）	cōngmáng	4-2
聪明	（形）	cōngming	2-4
从	（介）	cóng	2-9
从……起		cóng…qǐ	6-6
从此	（副）	cóngcǐ	5-9
从来	（副）	cónglái	4-6
从前	（名）	cóngqián	5-7
粗	（形）	cū	6-2
粗心	（形）	cūxīn	4-9
粗重	（形）	cūzhòng	6-2
醋	（名）	cù	6-1
催	（动）	cuī	5-9
村（子）	（名）	cūn(zi)	5-7
存	（动）	cún	3-8
存折	（名）	cúnzhé	5-9
错	（形）	cuò	1-5
错误	（名）	cuòwù	5-10
		D	
答应	（动）	dāying	4-5
达到	（动）	dádào	6-5
答案	（名）	dá'àn	5-2
打	（动）	dǎ	2-9
打扮	（动）	dǎban	5-1
打的	（动）	dǎdī	4-4
打电话		dǎ diànhuà	3-1
打搅	（动）	dǎjiǎo	6-4
打开	（动）	dǎkāi	3-5
打篮球		dǎ lánqiú	3-8
打扰	（动）	dǎrǎo	6-4
打扫	（动）	dǎsǎo	2-6
打算	（动）	dǎsuàn	5-2
打太极拳		dǎ tàijíquán	3-10
打招呼		dǎ zhāohu	5-3
打折	（动）	dǎzhé	3-3
打着灯笼也难找		dǎzhe dēnglong yě nán zhǎo	4-8
打针	（动）	dǎzhēn	2-9
打字	（动）	dǎzì	4-1
大	（形）	dà	2-3
大便	（动、名）	dàbiàn	3-4
大概	（副）	dàgài	5-10
大家	（代）	dàjiā	3-7
大使	（名）	dàshǐ	6-2
大使馆	（名）	dàshǐguǎn	6-2
大寿	（名）	dàshòu	5-7
大熊猫	（名）	dàxióngmāo	4-3
大学	（名）	dàxué	2-1
大约	（副）	dàyuē	4-9
呆	（形）	dāi	5-4
待	（动）	dāi	6-8
大夫	（名）	dàifu	2-1
代	（动）	dài	4-9
代	（名）	dài	4-8
代表	（动、名）	dàibiǎo	2-7

代替	（动）	dàitì	5-6
带	（动）	dài	2-8
戴	（动）	dài	5-2
担心	（动）	dānxīn	6-9
单	（形）	dān	2-2
单	（量）	dān	6-10
单车	（名）	dānchē	4-9
单间	（名）	dānjiān	5-7
单人间	（名）	dānrénjiān	2-3
单位	（名）	dānwèi	5-1
单子	（名）	dānzi	3-8
耽误	（动）	dānwu	3-1
但	（连）	dàn	3-10
但是	（连）	dànshì	3-10
淡	（形）	dàn	6-1
蛋	（名）	dàn	5-7
蛋糕	（名）	dàngāo	2-6
当	（动）	dāng	2-5
当地	（名）	dāngdì	4-5
当然	（副）	dāngrán	2-8
当时	（名）	dāngshí	4-2
当天	（名）	dàngtiān	6-4
当作	（动）	dàngzuò	4-10
倒	（动）	dǎo	5-8
倒霉	（形）	dǎoméi	5-9
到	（动）	dào	1-8
到处	（副）	dàochù	2-9
到达	（动）	dàodá	5-5
到底	（副）	dàodǐ	5-10
到期	（动）	dàoqī	5-2
倒	（副）	dào	4-4
道	（量）	dào	5-5
道德	（名）	dàodé	6-5
道理	（名）	dàolǐ	5-3
道路	（名）	dàolù	5-6

道歉	（动）	dàoqiàn	4-2
得到	（动）	dédào	5-1
得名	（动）	démíng	6-6
地	（助）	de	3-10
的	（助）	de	1-4
的话	（助）	dehuà	4-9
得	（助）	de	2-6
得	（能动）	děi	1-7
灯	（名）	dēng	4-8
灯笼	（名）	dēnglong	4-8
登	（动）	dēng	5-5
等	（动）	děng	2-10
等	（助）	děng	5-4
等待	（动）	děngdài	5-4
低	（形）	dī	3-2
的确	（副）	díquè	4-6
地	（名）	dì	2-8
地点	（名）	dìdiǎn	4-1
地方	（名）	dìfang	2-8
地理	（名）	dìlǐ	4-8
地球	（名）	dìqiú	5-5
地区	（名）	dìqū	6-1
地毯	（名）	dìtǎn	4-7
地铁	（名）	dìtiě	4-4
地图	（名）	dìtú	2-2
地下	（名）	dìxià	4-4
地址	（名）	dìzhǐ	5-9
弟弟	（名）	dìdi	2-1
递	（动）	dì	5-6
第		dì	4-2
点	（量）	diǎn	2-4
点	（动）	diǎn	4-4
点播	（动）	diǎnbō	6-10
点歌		diǎn gē	6-10
点头	（动）	diǎntóu	5-10

点心	（名）	diǎnxin	3-6
电	（名）	diàn	2-8
电车	（名）	diànchē	4-4
电灯	（名）	diàndēng	4-8
电动车	（名）	diàndòngchē	5-8
电话	（名）	diànhuà	3-1
电脑	（名）	diànnǎo	3-10
电扇	（名）	diànshàn	3-4
电视	（名）	diànshì	3-10
电视机	（名）	diànshìjī	5-9
电台	（名）	diàntái	6-10
电影	（名）	diànyǐng	2-8
电影院	（名）	diànyǐngyuàn	2-8
店	（名）	diàn	5-3
雕塑	（名）	diāosù	6-8
掉	（动）	diào	4-4
丁	（名）	dīng	4-6
丁字路口		dīngzì lùkǒu	4-9
顶	（名）	dǐng	3-8
顶	（量）	dǐng	5-2
订	（动）	dìng	2-3
定	（动）	dìng	3-8
丢	（动）	diū	4-9
东	（名）	dōng	3-1
东方	（名）	dōngfāng	3-6
东面	（名）	dōngmiàn	4-2
东坡肉	（名）	dōngpōròu	4-5
东西	（名）	dōngxi	2-6
冬季	（名）	dōngjì	2-3
冬天	（名）	dōngtiān	2-3
懂	（动）	dǒng	2-4
动身	（动）	dòngshēn	4-3
动物	（名）	dòngwù	4-3
动物园	（名）	dòngwùyuán	4-3

动作	（名）	dòngzuò	2-6
洞	（名）	dòng	6-8
洞窟	（名）	dòngkū	6-8
都	（副）	dōu	1-9
都		dū	6-3
毒	（名）	dú	6-7
读	（动）	dú	1-5
肚子	（名）	dùzi	2-9
度	（量）	dù	3-2
度过	（动）	dùguò	3-10
端	（动）	duān	4-7
短	（形）	duǎn	3-10
短期	（形）	duǎnqī	3-10
短信	（名）	duǎnxìn	5-8
段	（量）	duàn	5-5
断	（动）	duàn	5-8
锻炼	（动）	duànliàn	5-6
队	（名）	duì	3-1
对	（形）	duì	2-1
对	（介）	duì	2-5
对	（动）	duì	3-1
对……来说		duì…lái shuō	6-3
对不起	（动）	duìbuqǐ	1-5
对面	（名）	duìmiàn	3-2
对象	（名）	duìxiàng	5-1
兑换	（动）	duìhuàn	3-8
炖牛肉	（名）	dùnniúròu	1-4
顿	（量）	dùn	5-7
多	（形）	duō	1-6
多	（副）	duō	2-7
多少	（代）	duōshao	2-2
多子多福		duōzǐ duōfú	4-8
朵	（量）	duǒ	6-4
躲	（动）	duǒ	6-10

E			
饿	（形）	è	4-9
儿子	（名）	érzi	2-4
而	（连）	ér	5-5
而且	（连）	érqiě	4-1
耳环	（名）	ěrhuán	5-9
二	（数）	èr	1-1
二环路		èr-huánlù	4-9
F			
发	（动）	fā	2-1
发愁	（动）	fāchóu	6-10
发达	（形）	fādá	5-6
发烧	（动）	fāshāo	2-9
发生	（动）	fāshēng	5-8
发现	（动）	fāxiàn	5-1
发言	（动、名）	fāyán	3-7
发炎	（动）	fāyán	3-4
发音	（名）	fāyīn	1-10
发展	（动）	fāzhǎn	5-10
法律	（名）	fǎlǜ	3-8
法学	（名）	fǎxué	6-7
翻译	（名）	fānyì	2-5
烦	（形、动）	fán	6-9
反对	（动）	fǎnduì	6-5
反映	（动）	fǎnyìng	6-5
反正	（副）	fǎnzhèng	5-10
饭	（名）	fàn	1-4
饭店	（名）	fàndiàn	4-5
饭馆儿	（名）	fànguǎnr	4-5
方	（形）	fāng	6-1
方便	（形）	fāngbiàn	2-4
方法	（名）	fāngfǎ	1-10
方面	（名）	fāngmiàn	2-5

方向	（名）	fāngxiàng	4-9
房	（名）	fáng	4-7
房东	（名）	fángdōng	6-9
房间	（名）	fángjiān	2-3
访问	（动）	fǎngwèn	4-3
放	（动）	fàng	4-2
放假	（动）	fàngjià	5-6
放心	（动）	fàngxīn	3-1
飞	（动）	fēi	4-6
飞船	（名）	fēichuán	5-4
飞机	（名）	fēijī	3-4
飞快	（形）	fēikuài	5-10
非	（动）	fēi	5-5
非……不可		fēi…bù kě	6-9
非常	（副）	fēicháng	2-6
肥	（形）	féi	4-5
肺炎	（名）	fèiyán	6-9
费	（名）	fèi	3-5
费用	（名）	fèiyong	6-3
分	（量）	fēn	3-1
分	（动）	fēn	6-4
分别	（动）	fēnbié	5-9
分不开		fēn bu kāi	6-4
分开	（动）	fēnkāi	6-4
分配	（动）	fēnpèi	6-3
份	（量）	fèn	6-1
丰富	（形）	fēngfù	6-6
丰盛	（形）	fēngshèng	6-9
风	（名）	fēng	3-4
风景	（名）	fēngjǐng	6-3
风俗	（名）	fēngsú	6-6
风味	（名）	fēngwèi	4-5
风雨交加		fēngyǔ jiāojiā	6-9
封	（量）	fēng	2-1

佛	（名）	fó	6-8
佛像	（名）	fóxiàng	6-8
否认	（动）	fǒurèn	5-10
夫妇	（名）	fūfù	4-7
扶	（动）	fú	6-4
服务	（动）	fúwù	2-3
服务员	（名）	fúwùyuán	2-3
浮	（动）	fú	6-7
幅	（量）	fú	2-6
福	（名）	fú	4-7
抚摸	（动）	fǔmō	5-5
斧子	（名）	fǔzi	5-9
辅导	（动）	fǔdǎo	2-4
父母	（名）	fùmǔ	5-2
父亲	（名）	fùqin	3-2
付	（动）	fù	2-2
负责	（动）	fùzé	6-9
负责人	（名）	fùzérén	6-9
附件	（名）	fùjiàn	3-10
附近	（名）	fùjìn	1-5
复		fù	6-4
复活	（动）	fùhuó	6-4
复习	（动）	fùxí	1-7
副	（形）	fù	2-1
富	（形）	fù	6-10
富有	（动）	fùyǒu	4-1
腹	（名）	fù	4-10
腹泻	（动）	fùxiè	4-10
G			
该	（能动）	gāi	1-9
改	（动）	gǎi	5-10
改变	（动）	gǎibiàn	3-9
改进	（动）	gǎijìn	3-7
改善	（动）	gǎishàn	5-6
改造	（动）	gǎizào	6-6
改正	（动）	gǎizhèng	5-10
干	（形）	gān	6-1
干净	（形）	gānjìng	2-6
干涉	（动）	gānshè	6-10
赶紧	（副）	gǎnjǐn	6-5
赶快	（副）	gǎnkuài	6-2
敢	（能动）	gǎn	4-6
感到	（动）	gǎndào	5-2
感动	（形）	gǎndòng	4-2
感冒	（名、动）	gǎnmào	3-4
感情	（名）	gǎnqíng	6-10
感受	（名）	gǎnshòu	5-7
感谢	（动）	gǎnxiè	2-5
感兴趣		gǎn xìngqù	6-6
干	（动）	gàn	4-1
干吗	（代）	gànmá	3-8
刚	（副）	gāng	2-2
刚才	（名）	gāngcái	4-4
钢笔	（名）	gāngbǐ	2-2
高	（形）	gāo	3-2
高大	（形）	gāodà	5-8
高尔夫球	（名）	gāo'ěrfūqiú	4-5
高峰	（名）	gāofēng	6-2
高尚	（形）	gāoshàng	6-5
高铁	（名）	gāotiě	4-3
高兴	（形）	gāoxìng	1-8
搞	（动）	gǎo	6-10
告辞	（动）	gàocí	6-4
告诉	（动）	gàosu	3-8
哥哥	（名）	gēge	1-9
歌曲	（名）	gēqǔ	3-10
隔	（动）	gé	4-7
个	（量）	gè	1-8

个儿	（名）	gèr	6-3
个子	（名）	gèzi	4-8
各	（代）	gè	4-3
各种各样		gè zhǒng gè yàng	6-1
给	（动）	gěi	1-3
给	（介）	gěi	2-1
给	（助）	gěi	5-9
根	（量）	gēn	6-1
根本	（副）	gēnběn	6-2
跟	（介）	gēn	1-10
更换	（动）	gēnghuàn	5-3
更	（副）	gèng	2-4
工厂	（名）	gōngchǎng	2-1
工程	（名）	gōngchéng	5-10
工程师	（名）	gōngchéngshī	5-10
工地	（名）	gōngdì	5-10
工人	（名）	gōngrén	2-1
工作	（名）	gōngzuò	2-1
公安	（名）	gōng'ān	5-9
公安局	（名）	gōng'ānjú	5-9
公公	（名）	gōnggong	6-5
公共	（形）	gōnggòng	2-8
公共汽车		gōnggòng qìchē	2-8
公斤	（量）	gōngjīn	5-2
公里	（量）	gōnglǐ	5-2
公司	（名）	gōngsī	2-1
公务员	（名）	gōngwùyuán	2-5
公元	（名）	gōngyuán	6-8
公园儿	（名）	gōngyuánr	1-9
功能	（名）	gōngnéng	6-7
宫保鸡丁		gōngbǎo jīdīng	4-6
宫殿	（名）	gōngdiàn	6-10
共	（副）	gòng	4-1
共同	（副、形）	gòngtóng	3-10
共享	（动）	gòngxiǎng	4-9
共享单车		gòngxiǎng dānchē	4-9
贡献	（名）	gòngxiàn	4-3
狗	（名）	gǒu	2-1
够	（动）	gòu	3-9
估计	（动）	gūjì	5-6
姑姑	（名）	gūgu	4-7
姑娘	（名）	gūniang	2-9
古	（形）	gǔ	5-8
古代	（名）	gǔdài	5-2
古都	（名）	gǔdū	6-3
古迹	（名）	gǔjì	4-3
古老	（形）	gǔlǎo	3-6
故事	（名）	gùshi	3-8
瓜	（名）	guā	5-3
刮风	（动）	guāfēng	3-4
挂	（动）	guà	4-7
挂号	（动）	guàhào	3-5
拐	（动）	guǎi	4-9
怪	（形）	guài	2-6
怪不得	（副）	guàibude	2-6
关	（动）	guān	2-7
关	（名）	guān	5-5
关系	（名）	guānxi	2-6
关心	（动）	guānxīn	3-7
关于	（介）	guānyú	4-3
关照	（动）	guānzhào	4-5
关注	（动）	guānzhù	3-3
观点	（名）	guāndiǎn	5-10
观念	（名）	guānniàn	4-8
观众	（名）	guānzhòng	3-1
官	（名）	guān	6-5
管	（名、动）	guǎn	4-8
罐头	（名）	guàntou	5-6

光	（副）	guāng	5-2
光	（名）	guāng	5-4
光	（形）	guāng	6-10
广播	（动、名）	guǎngbō	4-1
广泛	（形）	guǎngfàn	6-9
逛	（动）	guàng	2-10
归		guī	6-10
规定	（名）	guīdìng	3-8
柜子	（名）	guìzi	5-9
贵	（形）	guì	1-3
贵姓	（名）	guìxìng	1-3
跪	（动）	guì	6-8
国	（名）	guó	1-4
国产	（形）	guóchǎn	3-3
国际	（形）	guójì	5-1
国家	（名）	guójiā	3-2
国外	（名）	guówài	6-3
果然	（副）	guǒrán	6-1
果园	（名）	guǒyuán	2-8
果汁儿	（名）	guǒzhīr	4-6
过	（动）	guò	2-7
过错	（名）	guòcuò	4-4
过去	（名）	guòqù	4-8
过	（助）	guo	4-3

H

哈哈	（叹）	hāhā	1-6
哈密瓜	（名）	hāmìguā	6-8
还	（副）	hái	1-7
还是	（连）	háishi	2-3
还是	（副）	háishi	2-10
孩子	（名）	háizi	2-10
海	（名）	hǎi	3-5
海棠	（名）	hǎitáng	5-4
海员	（名）	hǎiyuán	6-4
海运	（动）	hǎiyùn	3-5
害怕	（动）	hàipà	6-4
喊	（动）	hǎn	2-7
汉学	（名）	hànxué	3-6
汗	（名）	hàn	4-6
行家	（名）	hángjia	3-3
行业	（名）	hángyè	6-6
航空	（动）	hángkōng	3-5
好	（形）	hǎo	1-1
好吃	（形）	hǎochī	2-3
好处	（名）	hǎochù	2-10
好汉	（名）	hǎohàn	5-5
好几	（数）	hǎojǐ	5-1
好久	（形）	hǎojiǔ	1-7
好看	（形）	hǎokàn	1-9
好像	（副）	hǎoxiàng	3-6
号	（名）	hào	2-3
号码	（名）	hàomǎ	4-2
好	（动）	hào	5-1
喝	（动）	hē	1-3
合	（动）	hé	2-10
合格	（形）	hégé	5-3
合理	（形）	hélǐ	5-3
合适	（形）	héshì	2-3
合影	（名）	héyǐng	4-7
合住	（动）	hézhù	2-10
和	（连、介）	hé	1-9
和气	（形）	héqi	6-2
河	（名）	hé	2-8
盒儿	（名）	hér	4-4
盒子	（名）	hézi	5-3
贺卡	（名）	hèkǎ	3-5
黑	（形）	hēi	6-2
黑板	（名）	hēibǎn	2-2
很	（副）	hěn	1-4

红	（形）	hóng	1-9
红茶	（名）	hóngchá	3-3
红绿灯	（名）	hóng-lǜdēng	4-9
红烧	（动）	hóngshāo	4-5
红烧猪手		hóngshāo zhūshǒu	4-5
猴	（名）	hóu	2-6
后	（名）	hòu	2-8
后边	（名）	hòubian	2-8
后代	（名）	hòudài	5-5
后悔	（动）	hòuhuǐ	6-5
后来	（名）	hòulái	3-8
后面	（名）	hòumiàn	4-2
后年	（名）	hòunián	3-2
后天	（名）	hòutiān	2-3
厚	（形）	hòu	5-3
呼	（动）	hū	6-6
呼吸	（动）	hūxī	6-6
忽然	（副）	hūrán	5-1
胡同	（名）	hútòng	6-6
壶	（名）	hú	6-7
湖	（名）	hú	4-3
互相	（副）	hùxiāng	1-8
户	（量）	hù	6-4
护士	（名）	hùshi	4-10
护照	（名）	hùzhào	3-8
花	（动）	huā	3-3
花草	（名）	huācǎo	4-10
花茶	（名）	huāchá	6-7
花儿	（名）	huār	1-9
花生米	（名）	huāshēngmǐ	4-6
花园	（名）	huāyuán	4-10
划	（动）	huá	4-3
滑冰	（动）	huábīng	3-2
化解	（动）	huàjiě	6-9
化学	（名）	huàxué	6-8
化验	（动）	huàyàn	3-4
画	（动）	huà	2-9
画报	（名）	huàbào	3-5
画儿	（名）	huàr	2-6
话	（名）	huà	2-7
话剧	（名）	huàjù	5-7
话题	（名）	huàtí	4-8
怀疑	（动）	huáiyí	5-9
坏	（形）	huài	5-8
欢快	（形）	huānkuài	5-6
欢乐	（形）	huānlè	6-8
欢迎	（动）	huānyíng	1-8
还	（动）	huán	3-8
环	（名）	huán	4-9
环境	（名）	huánjìng	2-8
环路	（名）	huánlù	4-9
缓和	（形）	huǎnhé	6-5
换	（动）	huàn	3-8
黄	（形）	huáng	1-9
灰	（形）	huī	6-6
灰色	（名）	huīsè	6-6
恢复	（动）	huīfù	2-9
回	（动）	huí	1-7
回	（量）	huí	3-8
回忆	（动）	huíyì	6-3
会	（能动）	huì	2-8
会	（名）	huì	5-8
会议	（名）	huìyì	5-6
婚姻	（名）	hūnyīn	5-1
馄饨	（名）	húntun	6-1
活	（形）	huó	5-1
活动	（名）	huódòng	6-9
活儿	（名）	huór	5-7
火车	（名）	huǒchē	4-3

伙伴	（名）	huǒbàn	5-9
或	（连）	huò	2-10
或者	（连）	huòzhě	2-10
货	（名）	huò	3-9
J			
几乎	（副）	jīhū	4-5
机场	（名）	jīchǎng	3-3
机会	（名）	jīhuì	3-7
机票	（名）	jīpiào	3-6
机器	（名）	jīqì	3-8
鸡	（名）	jī	4-6
鸡蛋	（名）	jīdàn	5-7
鸡丁	（名）	jīdīng	4-6
积极	（形）	jījí	3-7
基本	（形、副）	jīběn	5-10
基础	（名）	jīchǔ	3-8
激动	（形）	jīdòng	5-9
及格	（动）	jígé	3-4
及时	（副）	jíshí	5-4
吉利	（形）	jílì	2-7
级	（名）	jí	5-5
极	（副）	jí	1-7
极了		jí le	1-7
急	（形）	jí	4-8
急救	（动）	jíjiù	6-9
急忙	（副）	jímáng	5-10
急事	（名）	jíshì	4-8
急性	（形）	jíxìng	4-10
急诊室	（名）	jízhěnshì	4-10
集合	（动）	jíhé	6-9
集体	（名）	jítǐ	6-9
集邮	（动）	jíyóu	3-5
几	（代）	jǐ	2-1
挤	（形）	jǐ	2-10

计划	（动、名）	jìhuà	6-1
记	（动）	jì	1-5
记得	（动）	jìde	4-5
记录	（动）	jìlù	6-6
纪律	（名）	jìlǜ	4-9
纪念	（动、名）	jìniàn	3-5
纪念品	（名）	jìniànpǐn	5-9
纪念日	（名）	jìniànrì	3-10
技术	（名）	jìshù	6-8
系	（动）	jì	6-2
季	（名）	jì	3-2
季节	（名）	jìjié	3-2
既……也……		jì…yě…	4-9
既……又……		jì…yòu…	4-5
既然	（连）	jìrán	5-3
继续	（动）	jìxù	6-5
寄	（动）	jì	2-6
寄件人	（名）	jìjiànrén	5-9
寂寞	（形）	jìmò	4-10
加	（动）	jiā	6-6
加强	（动）	jiāqiáng	3-7
佳	（形）	jiā	6-1
家	（名）	jiā	1-9
……家		…jiā	3-6
家庭	（名）	jiātíng	2-1
家务	（名）	jiāwù	4-8
家乡	（名）	jiāxiāng	6-3
假	（形）	jiǎ	2-10
价	（名）	jià	3-9
价格	（名）	jiàgé	3-9
价钱	（名）	jiàqian	6-4
价值	（名）	jiàzhí	3-9
架	（量）	jià	3-4
假日	（名）	jiàrì	4-3

嫁	（动）	jià	6-1
坚持	（动）	jiānchí	6-9
间	（量）	jiān	4-7
肩	（名）	jiān	5-5
拣	（动）	jiǎn	6-3
检查	（动）	jiǎnchá	4-10
减	（动）	jiǎn	5-6
减肥	（动）	jiǎnféi	5-6
减少	（动）	jiǎnshǎo	5-6
简单	（形）	jiǎndān	2-3
简直	（副）	jiǎnzhí	6-7
见	（动）	jiàn	1-6
见面	（动）	jiànmiàn	5-1
件	（量）	jiàn	2-3
建	（动）	jiàn	4-5
建议	（动）	jiànyì	3-6
建筑	（动、名）	jiànzhù	4-5
健康	（形）	jiànkāng	2-7
江	（名）	jiāng	6-3
将	（副）	jiāng	4-1
讲	（动）	jiǎng	3-4
讲究	（动）	jiǎngjiu	6-5
讲台	（名）	jiǎngtái	3-7
讲座	（名）	jiǎngzuò	4-1
酱油	（名）	jiàngyóu	6-1
交	（动）	jiāo	2-1
交换	（动）	jiāohuàn	2-4
交际	（动）	jiāojì	5-10
交流	（动）	jiāoliú	6-7
交通	（名）	jiāotōng	4-9
郊		jiāo	2-8
郊区	（名）	jiāoqū	2-8
教	（动）	jiāo	2-4
角	（量）	jiǎo	3-3
狡辩	（动）	jiǎobiàn	4-4

饺子	（名）	jiǎozi	4-1
脚	（名）	jiǎo	6-4
叫	（动）	jiào	1-3
叫	（介）	jiào	5-9
叫号	（动）	jiàohào	3-8
教师	（名）	jiàoshī	2-5
教室	（名）	jiàoshì	2-4
教授	（名）	jiàoshòu	3-9
教学	（名）	jiàoxué	2-1
教育	（动、名）	jiàoyù	6-4
阶段	（名）	jiēduàn	2-4
接	（动）	jiē	2-10
接受	（动）	jiēshòu	4-2
接着	（副）	jiēzhe	5-5
街	（名）	jiē	2-8
街道	（名）	jiēdào	6-6
节目	（名）	jiémù	3-9
节约	（动）	jiéyuē	6-9
洁白	（形）	jiébái	6-3
结	（动）	jié	3-10
结果	（名）	jiéguǒ	3-4
结果	（连）	jiéguǒ	5-8
结婚	（动）	jiéhūn	3-6
结束	（动）	jiéshù	2-5
结账	（动）	jiézhàng	4-6
姐姐	（名）	jiějie	2-1
解毒	（动）	jiědú	6-7
解饿	（动）	jiě'è	5-2
解渴	（动）	jiěkě	5-2
解释	（动）	jiěshì	5-9
解围	（动）	jiěwéi	6-5
介绍	（动）	jièshào	1-8
介意	（动）	jièyì	6-2
戒	（动）	jiè	4-4
戒指	（名）	jièzhi	5-9

借	（动）	jiè	3-6
斤	（量）	jīn	3-3
今年	（名）	jīnnián	2-9
今天	（名）	jīntiān	2-1
金	（名）	jīn	3-10
金婚	（名）	jīnhūn	3-10
金子	（名）	jīnzi	3-10
仅	（副）	jǐn	6-3
紧张	（形）	jǐnzhāng	1-7
尽力	（动）	jìnlì	5-1
尽头	（名）	jìntóu	5-5
进	（动）	jìn	2-6
进步	（动）	jìnbù	2-5
进口	（动）	jìnkǒu	3-3
进行	（动）	jìnxíng	2-5
进修	（动）	jìnxiū	6-1
近	（形）	jìn	1-5
京剧	（名）	jīngjù	3-8
经常	（副）	jīngcháng	3-6
经过	（动）	jīngguò	3-9
经济	（名）	jīngjì	5-7
经理	（名）	jīnglǐ	2-1
经历	（名）	jīnglì	5-6
经商	（动）	jīngshāng	2-5
经验	（名）	jīngyàn	6-4
惊叹号	（名）	jīngtànhào	5-5
精彩	（形）	jīngcǎi	5-3
精神	（形）	jīngshen	5-1
精神病	（名）	jīngshénbìng	6-9
精致	（形）	jīngzhì	6-1
井	（名）	jǐng	6-6
警察	（名）	jǐngchá	3-3
敬	（动）	jìng	6-7
究竟	（副）	jiūjìng	6-3
九	（数）	jiǔ	1-1

久	（形）	jiǔ	1-7
酒	（名）	jiǔ	3-6
酒店	（名）	jiǔdiàn	5-7
旧	（形）	jiù	3-4
救	（动）	jiù	5-1
就	（副）	jiù	2-2
舅舅	（名）	jiùjiu	4-7
舅妈	（名）	jiùmā	4-7
鞠躬	（动）	jūgōng	6-2
局	（名）	jú	5-9
橘子	（名）	júzi	5-3
举	（动）	jǔ	3-7
举办	（动）	jǔbàn	3-6
举行	（动）	jǔxíng	4-2
句	（名）	jù	1-10
句子	（名）	jùzi	1-10
俱	（副）	jù	6-1
剧场	（名）	jùchǎng	2-8
据	（介）	jù	5-6
据说	（动）	jùshuō	6-5
聚会	（动）	jùhuì	6-7
卷	（量）	juǎn	5-10
觉得	（动）	juéde	1-10
决定	（动）	juédìng	4-4
		K	
咖啡	（名）	kāfēi	4-1
卡拉 OK		kǎlā OK	5-7
开	（动）	kāi	2-7
开会	（动）	kāihuì	5-8
开始	（动）	kāishǐ	2-4
开水	（名）	kāishuǐ	3-4
开玩笑		kāi wánxiào	3-6
开心	（形）	kāixīn	5-4
开学	（动）	kāixué	5-6

开演	（动）	kāiyǎn	4-6
开凿	（动）	kāizáo	6-8
看	（动）	kàn	1-6
看不起	（动）	kànbuqǐ	5-3
看来	（动）	kànlái	3-1
看望	（动）	kànwàng	4-9
看作	（动）	kànzuò	5-4
考	（动）	kǎo	3-4
考虑	（动）	kǎolǜ	2-3
考试	（动）	kǎoshì	3-4
烤	（动）	kǎo	4-3
烤鸭	（名）	kǎoyā	4-3
科	（名）	kē	4-10
科学	（名、形）	kēxué	6-9
科长	（名）	kēzhǎng	6-9
棵	（量）	kē	4-10
咳嗽	（动）	késou	2-9
可	（连）	kě	1-10
可	（能动）	kě	5-8
可……了		kě…le	4-5
可爱	（形）	kě'ài	2-6
可能	（能动、名）	kěnéng	3-3
可是	（连）	kěshì	1-10
可以	（能动）	kěyǐ	2-2
渴	（形）	kě	1-3
克服	（动）	kèfú	5-1
刻	（量）	kè	3-1
刻苦	（形）	kèkǔ	5-1
客气	（动、形）	kèqi	1-8
客人	（名）	kèren	4-2
客厅	（名）	kètīng	4-7
课	（名）	kè	1-7
课本	（名）	kèběn	4-8
课间	（名）	kèjiān	4-9

课堂	（名）	kètáng	5-10
课文	（名）	kèwén	1-5
肯定	（副）	kěndìng	5-8
空气	（名）	kōngqì	5-1
空调	（名）	kōngtiáo	2-3
空运	（动）	kōngyùn	3-5
空儿	（名）	kòngr	1-8
空隙	（名）	kòngxì	5-6
口	（量）	kǒu	2-1
口袋	（名）	kǒudai	4-9
口感	（名）	kǒugǎn	3-3
口试	（动）	kǒushì	1-10
口味	（名）	kǒuwèi	6-1
口语	（名）	kǒuyǔ	2-4
扣子	（名）	kòuzi	5-6
哭	（动）	kū	4-8
苦	（形）	kǔ	4-10
裤子	（名）	kùzi	3-9
夸奖	（动）	kuājiǎng	3-6
夸张	（形）	kuāzhāng	6-6
块	（量）	kuài	1-4
快	（形）	kuài	2-5
快餐	（名）	kuàicān	6-1
快递	（名）	kuàidì	4-9
快乐	（形）	kuàilè	2-7
筷子	（名）	kuàizi	3-8
宽	（形）	kuān	3-2
筐	（名）	kuāng	5-3
矿泉水	（名）	kuàngquán-shuǐ	6-7
困	（形）	kùn	4-9
困难	（名）	kùnnan	5-1
L			
拉	（动）	lā	4-8
拉活儿	（动）	lāhuór	6-10

蜡烛	（名）	làzhú	2-6
辣	（形）	là	4-5
啦	（助）	la	2-6
来	（动）	lái	1-4
来	（名）	lái	5-5
来不及	（动）	láibují	3-8
来着	（助）	láizhe	5-7
栏	（名）	lán	5-9
栏目	（名）	lánmù	6-10
蓝	（形）	lán	1-9
篮球	（名）	lánqiú	3-8
浪费	（动）	làngfèi	3-9
浪漫	（形）	làngmàn	4-1
劳动	（动、名）	láodòng	6-4
劳驾	（动）	láojià	2-2
老		lǎo	2-4
老	（形）	lǎo	2-7
老百姓	（名）	lǎobǎixìng	6-7
老板	（名）	lǎobǎn	3-3
老大爷	（名）	lǎodàye	5-6
老婆	（名）	lǎopo	5-1
老人	（名）	lǎorén	2-7
老师	（名）	lǎoshī	1-3
老是	（副）	lǎoshì	5-7
老实	（形）	lǎoshi	5-6
姥姥	（名）	lǎolao	4-7
姥爷	（名）	lǎoye	4-7
了	（助）	le	1-3
类	（名、量）	lèi	6-1
累	（形）	lèi	1-3
冷	（形）	lěng	2-3
愣	（动）	lèng	6-2
厘米	（量）	límǐ	5-2
离	（动）	lí	2-8
离婚	（动）	líhūn	4-4

礼貌	（形、名）	lǐmào	6-2
礼堂	（名）	lǐtáng	5-6
礼物	（名）	lǐwù	2-6
里	（量）	lǐ	1-9
里	（名）	lǐ	1-9
里边	（名）	lǐbian	1-9
里弄	（名）	lǐlòng	6-6
里面	（名）	lǐmiàn	4-2
理	（动）	lǐ	6-2
理解	（动）	lǐjiě	5-2
理想	（名）	lǐxiǎng	5-5
力气	（名）	lìqi	5-3
历史	（名）	lìshǐ	2-5
厉害	（形）	lìhai	3-4
立交桥	（名）	lìjiāoqiáo	5-6
立刻	（副）	lìkè	5-8
利息	（名）	lìxī	6-10
利用	（动）	lìyòng	6-9
利于	（动）	lìyú	4-10
例如	（动）	lìrú	6-5
俩	（数量）	liǎ	4-3
连	（动）	lián	3-10
连……也/都……		lián…yě/dōu…	4-6
连接	（动）	liánjiē	5-5
连忙	（副）	liánmáng	4-2
连声	（副）	liánshēng	6-4
联系	（动）	liánxì	6-2
脸	（名）	liǎn	3-2
脸色	（名）	liǎnsè	3-2
练	（动）	liàn	1-7
练习	（名）	liànxí	1-7
恋爱	（名、动）	liàn'ài	5-7
良	（形）	liáng	4-10
良药苦口利于病		liángyào kǔkǒu lìyú bìng	4-10

凉快	（形）	liángkuai	2-3
量	（动）	liáng	3-4
两	（数）	liǎng	2-2
两	（量）	liǎng	3-3
亮	（形）	liàng	5-4
辆	（量）	liàng	3-6
聊天儿	（动）	< 口 >liáotiānr	2-5
了	（动）	liǎo	5-1
了不起	（形）	liǎobuqǐ	6-5
了解	（动）	liǎojiě	2-5
瞭望台	（名）	liàowàngtái	5-5
邻居	（名）	línjū	5-7
灵	（形）	líng	4-4
灵感	（名）	línggǎn	6-8
聆听	（动）	língtīng	6-10
领	（动）	lǐng	5-8
领导	（名）	lǐngdǎo	5-3
另	（代）	lìng	5-2
另外	（连）	lìngwài	5-10
留	（动）	liú	4-3
留步	（动）	liúbù	4-2
留念	（动）	liúniàn	6-8
留学	（动）	liúxué	2-5
留学生	（名）	liúxuéshēng	2-5
流	（动）	liú	6-3
流利	（形）	liúlì	2-6
六	（数）	liù	1-1
龙	（名）	lóng	5-4
龙井	（名）	lóngjǐng	6-7
楼	（名）	lóu	1-8
楼梯	（名）	lóutī	6-9
录取	（动）	lùqǔ	6-10
录像	（动、名）	lùxiàng	5-7
录音	（名）	lùyīn	1-10
录音笔	（名）	lùyīnbǐ	3-4

路	（名）	lù	1-9
路口	（名）	lùkǒu	4-9
路况	（名）	lùkuàng	6-10
路上	（名）	lùshang	5-3
路线	（名）	lùxiàn	4-9
旅伴	（名）	lǚbàn	6-8
旅行	（动）	lǚxíng	2-5
旅行社	（名）	lǚxíngshè	5-1
旅游	（动）	lǚyóu	4-3
绿	（形）	lǜ	5-5
绿茶	（名）	lǜchá	3-3
乱	（形）	luàn	6-5
轮	（量）	lún	5-4
		M	
妈妈	（名）	māma	1-9
麻	（形）	má	4-6
麻烦	（动）	máfan	3-5
麻将	（名）	májiàng	5-7
马	（名）	mǎ	4-3
马路	（名）	mǎlù	4-9
马上	（副）	mǎshàng	4-7
骂	（动）	mà	4-8
吗	（助）	ma	1-3
嘛	（助）	ma	4-10
埋	（动）	mái	6-8
买	（动）	mǎi	1-6
买单	（动）	mǎidān	6-1
买卖	（名）	mǎimai	5-3
卖	（动）	mài	3-3
馒头	（名）	mántou	1-4
满	（形）	mǎn	4-6
满意	（动）	mǎnyì	4-6
满月	（动）	mǎnyuè	6-5
满足	（动）	mǎnzú	4-1

慢	（形）	màn	2-5
忙	（形）	máng	1-4
盲肠	（名）	mángcháng	4-10
盲肠炎	（名）	mángchángyán	4-10
毛	（量）	máo	3-3
毛	（名）	máo	6-6
毛病	（名）	máobìng	5-8
毛峰	（名）	máofēng	6-7
毛衣	（名）	máoyī	3-6
矛盾	（名、动）	máodùn	4-8
茅台酒	（名）	máotáijiǔ	3-6
冒	（动）	mào	4-1
冒火	（动）	màohuǒ	6-2
帽子	（名）	màozi	5-2
没	（动）	méi	1-7
没关系		méi guānxi	2-6
没有	（动）	méiyǒu	1-7
眉毛	（名）	méimao	6-3
每	（代）	měi	1-5
每天		měi tiān	1-5
美	（形）	měi	4-5
美好	（形）	měihǎo	3-10
美丽	（形）	měilì	5-4
美满	（形）	měimǎn	6-10
美食城	（名）	měishíchéng	4-5
美食家	（名）	měishíjiā	4-5
美术	（名）	měishù	6-8
美味佳肴		měiwèi jiāyáo	4-5
美元	（名）	měiyuán	2-3
妹妹	（名）	mèimei	2-1
门	（名）	mén	2-7
门口	（名）	ménkǒu	3-1
门诊部	（名）	ménzhěnbù	4-10
们		men	3-7
猛	（副）	měng	5-6
猛然	（副）	měngrán	6-2
梦	（动、名）	mèng	4-7
梦想	（名）	mèngxiǎng	5-5
迷	（动）	mí	3-1
……迷		…mí	3-1
米	（量）	mǐ	3-2
米饭	（名）	mǐfàn	1-4
秘密	（名）	mìmì	6-1
面	（名）	miàn	6-7
面包	（名）	miànbāo	3-6
面积	（名）	miànjī	5-6
面料	（名）	miànliào	3-9
面条儿	（名）	miàntiáor	4-1
面子	（名）	miànzi	5-10
苗条	（形）	miáotiao	6-3
秒	（量）	miǎo	3-2
民歌	（名）	míngē	5-4
民俗	（名）	mínsú	5-2
民族	（名）	mínzú	5-4
名称	（名）	míngchēng	6-6
名牌儿	（名）	míngpáir	3-9
名片	（名）	míngpiàn	4-2
名儿	（名）	míngr	4-5
名胜	（名）	míngshèng	4-3
名字	（名）	míngzi	1-8
明白	（形）	míngbai	2-10
明亮	（形）	míngliàng	5-4
明码标价		míngmǎ biāojià	3-9
明年	（名）	míngnián	3-2
明天	（名）	míngtiān	1-9
明信片	（名）	míngxìnpiàn	3-5
命	（名）	mìng	4-9
命名	（动）	mìngmíng	6-6
摸	（动）	mō	4-9
模仿	（动）	mófǎng	5-10

摩托车	（名）	mótuōchē	5-8
茉莉花	（名）	mòlìhuā	6-7
茉莉花茶	（名）	mòlìhuāchá	6-7
某	（代）	mǒu	3-9
母亲	（名）	mǔqin	2-9
木		mù	4-10
目的	（名）	mùdì	2-5
牧民	（名）	mùmín	6-7

N

拿	（动）	ná	3-3
拿……来说		ná…lái shuō	4-5
拿手	（形）	náshǒu	4-6
哪	（代）	nǎ	1-4
哪里	（代）	nǎli	3-5
哪儿	（代）	nǎr	1-7
那	（代）	nà	1-5
那	（连）	nà	3-9
那边	（名）	nàbian	1-5
那里	（代）	nàlǐ	5-10
那么	（代）	nàme	1-9
那儿	（代）	nàr	1-6
那样	（代）	nàyàng	5-4
哪	（助）	na	4-1
奶	（名）	nǎi	5-2
奶茶	（名）	nǎichá	6-7
奶奶	（名）	nǎinai	1-9
耐心	（形、名）	nàixīn	5-4
男	（形）	nán	1-5
男孩儿	（名）	nánháir	3-7
男人	（名）	〈口〉 nánren	4-8
男生	（名）	nánshēng	2-4
男声	（名）	nánshēng	6-2
南	（名）	nán	3-1
南方	（名）	nánfāng	2-5
南门	（名）	nánmén	3-1
南面	（名）	nánmiàn	4-2
难	（形）	nán	1-10
难得	（形）	nándé	6-5
难过	（形）	nánguò	5-9
难以忘怀		nányǐ wàng-huái	6-9
闹	（动、形）	nào	5-9
闹钟	（名）	nàozhōng	5-9
呢	（助）	ne	1-4
内		nèi	4-10
内科	（名）	nèikē	4-10
内容	（名）	nèiróng	5-2
能	（能动）	néng	2-5
你	（代）	nǐ	1-1
你们	（代）	nǐmen	1-2
年	（名）	nián	2-6
年代	（名）	niándài	5-6
年级	（名）	niánjí	2-2
年纪	（名）	niánjì	2-4
年龄	（名）	niánlíng	2-9
年轻	（形）	niánqīng	2-4
念	（动）	niàn	1-5
您	（代）	nín	1-2
牛毛	（名）	niúmáo	6-6
牛奶	（名）	niúnǎi	5-2
牛肉	（名）	niúròu	1-4
农历	（名）	nónglì	5-4
农贸市场		nóngmào shìchǎng	5-3
农民	（名）	nóngmín	5-8
浓	（形）	nóng	6-6
浓厚	（形）	nónghòu	6-6
弄	（动）	nòng	5-8
努力	（形）	nǔlì	3-2
暖和	（形）	nuǎnhuo	2-3

暖气	（名）	nuǎnqì	2-3
女	（形）	nǚ	1-5
女儿	（名）	nǚ'ér	2-4
女孩儿	（名）	nǚháir	3-7
女孩子	（名）	nǚháizi	2-9
女人	（名）	nǚrén	4-8
女生	（名）	nǚshēng	2-4
女声	（名）	nǚshēng	6-2
女士	（名）	nǚshì	3-9
P			
爬	（动）	pá	3-8
怕	（动）	pà	3-7
拍摄	（动）	pāishè	6-8
拍照	（动）	pāizhào	6-8
排	（动、名）	pái	6-1
排队	（动）	páiduì	6-1
排列	（动）	páiliè	6-6
排球	（名）	páiqiú	4-5
牌子	（名）	páizi	5-10
派	（动）	pài	4-9
盘	（量）	pán	4-6
盼	（动）	pàn	6-5
盼望	（动）	pànwàng	6-5
旁	（名）	páng	2-8
旁边	（名）	pángbiān	2-8
胖	（形）	pàng	4-1
跑	（动）	pǎo	2-6
陪	（动）	péi	4-7
陪伴	（动）	péibàn	6-9
佩服	（动）	pèifu	6-2
朋友	（名）	péngyou	1-4
碰	（动）	pèng	6-9
碰见	（动）	pèngjiàn	6-9
批	（量）	pī	3-9
批评	（动）	pīpíng	4-2
皮	（名）	pí	6-3
皮肤	（名）	pífū	6-3
皮鞋	（名）	píxié	3-3
啤酒	（名）	píjiǔ	3-6
脾气	（名）	píqi	6-4
匹	（量）	pǐ	5-8
偏	（副）	piān	6-8
偏偏	（副）	piānpiān	6-8
篇	（量）	piān	2-6
便宜	（形）	piányi	1-6
片	（名、量）	piàn	3-4
骗	（动）	piàn	3-3
票	（名）	piào	3-1
漂亮	（形）	piàoliang	2-7
……品		…pǐn	5-9
品尝	（动）	pǐncháng	4-5
聘请	（动）	pìnqǐng	4-1
乒乓球	（名）	pīngpāngqiú	4-5
平等	（形）	píngděng	4-8
平方	（名、量）	píngfāng	5-6
平方米	（量）	píngfāngmǐ	5-6
平静	（形）	píngjìng	6-2
平均	（动）	píngjūn	6-8
平时	（名）	píngshí	4-9
平台	（名）	píngtái	6-2
苹果	（名）	píngguǒ	2-3
瓶	（量）	píng	3-6
婆婆	（名）	pópo	6-5
破	（形、动）	pò	5-3
破坏	（动）	pòhuài	6-8
破旧	（形）	pòjiù	5-3
扑克	（名）	pūkè	5-7
铺	（动）	pū	4-7
葡萄	（名）	pútao	4-6

葡萄酒	（名）	pútaojiǔ	4-6
普洱茶	（名）	pǔ'ěrchá	3-3
普通	（形）	pǔtōng	5-2
普通话	（名）	pǔtōnghuà	5-2

Q

七	（数）	qī	1-1
沏	（动）	qī	4-7
妻管严		qīguǎnyán	4-8
妻子	（名）	qīzi	3-6
期	（名）	qī	5-2
期间	（名）	qījiān	5-10
其次	（代）	qícì	6-7
其实	（副）	qíshí	5-10
其他	（代）	qítā	6-9
其中	（名）	qízhōng	6-10
奇怪	（形）	qíguài	3-3
奇迹	（名）	qíjì	5-5
奇特	（形）	qítè	6-6
骑	（动）	qí	2-8
棋	（名）	qí	5-7
启发	（动）	qǐfā	6-8
起床	（动）	qǐchuáng	3-1
起名儿	（动）	qǐmíngr	6-5
气氛	（名）	qìfēn	5-6
气功	（名）	qìgōng	4-7
气管	（名）	qìguǎn	4-8
气管炎	（名）	qìguǎnyán	4-8
气温	（名）	qìwēn	3-2
汽车	（名）	qìchē	2-8
汽车站	（名）	qìchēzhàn	4-9
汽水儿	（名）	qìshuǐr	4-6
洽谈	（动）	qiàtán	6-7
千	（数）	qiān	3-2
千儿八百		qiān'er-bābǎi	5-7

千万	（副）	qiānwàn	4-9
迁居	（动）	qiānjū	6-3
铅笔	（名）	qiānbǐ	2-2
谦虚	（形）	qiānxū	4-1
签字	（动）	qiānzì	3-8
前	（名）	qián	1-8
前边	（名）	qiánbian	1-8
前面	（名）	qiánmiàn	4-2
前年	（名）	qiánnián	3-2
前天	（名）	qiántiān	2-3
钱	（名）	qián	2-2
钱包	（名）	qiánbāo	2-8
浅	（形）	qiǎn	6-2
强	（形）	qiáng	5-8
强调	（动）	qiángdiào	5-10
强壮	（形）	qiángzhuàng	5-8
墙	（名）	qiáng	2-8
敲	（动）	qiāo	2-7
桥	（名）	qiáo	3-7
瞧	（动）	qiáo	3-3
亲爱	（形）	qīn'ài	3-6
亲戚	（名）	qīnqi	5-7
亲切	（形）	qīnqiè	6-2
亲人	（名）	qīnrén	4-10
亲手	（副）	qīnshǒu	6-4
亲眼	（副）	qīnyǎn	6-8
亲自	（副）	qīnzì	6-6
琴	（名）	qín	6-8
青	（形）	qīng	4-6
青菜	（名）	qīngcài	4-6
轻	（形）	qīng	5-2
轻松	（形）	qīngsōng	4-2
清	（形）	qīng	6-3
清楚	（形）	qīngchu	2-6
清淡	（形）	qīngdàn	4-5

情景	（名）	qíngjǐng	6-8
情况	（名）	qíngkuàng	1-8
情人	（名）	qíngrén	3-6
晴	（形）	qíng	3-2
晴朗	（形）	qínglǎng	5-4
请	（动）	qǐng	1-8
请假	（动）	qǐngjià	3-7
请客	（动）	qǐngkè	2-2
请求	（动、名）	qǐngqiú	6-9
请示	（动）	qǐngshì	6-9
请问	（动）	qǐngwèn	1-8
庆祝	（动）	qìngzhù	3-6
穷	（形）	qióng	6-10
秋季	（名）	qiūjì	3-2
秋天	（名）	qiūtiān	3-2
球	（名）	qiú	3-1
区		qū	2-10
区别	（名）	qūbié	6-1
曲艺	（名）	qǔyì	6-7
取	（动）	qǔ	3-6
取得	（动）	qǔdé	3-7
娶	（动）	qǔ	5-7
去	（动）	qù	1-6
去年	（名）	qùnián	3-2
去世	（动）	qùshì	4-4
趣闻	（名）	qùwén	6-9
圈子	（名）	quānzi	6-10
全	（形）	quán	2-7
全家福	（名）	quánjiāfú	4-7
全面	（形）	quánmiàn	6-5
全体	（名）	quántǐ	6-10
泉	（名）	quán	6-7
拳	（名）	quán	3-10
缺	（动）	quē	3-4
缺点	（名）	quēdiǎn	5-10
缺少	（动）	quēshǎo	6-7
却	（副）	què	5-2
确实	（副）	quèshí	5-5
裙子	（名）	qúnzi	3-9
群	（量）	qún	5-8
R			
然后	（连）	ránhòu	3-8
嚷	（动）	rǎng	6-9
让	（动）	ràng	2-7
让	（介）	ràng	5-8
让座儿	（动）	ràngzuòr	5-6
绕	（动）	rào	5-5
热	（形）	rè	2-3
热乎乎	（形）	rèhūhū	5-1
热泪盈眶		rèlèi yíngkuàng	6-10
热烈	（形）	rèliè	6-10
热闹	（形）	rènao	4-7
热情	（形）	rèqíng	3-3
热心	（形）	rèxīn	5-1
人	（名）	rén	1-3
人家	（代）	rénjia	5-1
人口	（名）	rénkǒu	5-6
人类	（名）	rénlèi	5-5
人们	（名）	rénmen	3-4
人民币	（名）	rénmínbì	2-3
人生	（名）	rénshēng	4-3
人体	（名）	réntǐ	6-7
人为	（形）	rénwéi	6-8
人物	（名）	rénwù	6-6
认识	（动）	rènshi	1-4
认为	（动）	rènwéi	2-5
认真	（形）	rènzhēn	3-7
任何	（代）	rènhé	6-4
任意	（副）	rènyì	6-1

日	（名）	rì	2-9
日报	（名）	rìbào	4-2
日记	（名）	rìjì	5-5
日历	（名）	rìlì	3-2
日期	（名）	rìqī	5-3
日子	（名）	rìzi	5-8
容易	（形）	róngyì	1-10
肉	（名）	ròu	4-5
如	（连）	rú	5-3
如果	（连）	rúguǒ	5-3
如今	（名）	rújīn	6-10
如意	（动）	rúyì	2-7
软	（形）	ruǎn	5-7
弱	（形）	ruò	5-8
S			
洒	（动）	sǎ	5-4
赛	（动）	sài	3-1
三	（数）	sān	1-1
伞	（名）	sǎn	4-1
散	（动）	sàn	4-2
散步	（动）	sànbù	3-2
嗓子	（名）	sǎngzi	2-9
扫码	（动）	sǎomǎ	4-6
嫂子	（名）	sǎozi	1-9
色	（名）	sè	3-2
沙丁鱼	（名）	shādīngyú	5-6
沙发	（名）	shāfā	3-7
沙子	（名）	shāzi	6-8
傻	（形）	shǎ	5-1
山	（名）	shān	2-8
山泉	（名）	shānquán	6-7
山山水水		shānshānshuǐ-shuǐ	4-3
伤	（名、动）	shāng	5-10
商场	（名）	shāngchǎng	3-9
商店	（名）	shāngdiàn	1-6
商贩	（名）	shāngfàn	5-3
商量	（动）	shāngliang	3-8
上	（名）	shàng	1-6
上班	（动）	shàngbān	2-10
上边	（名）	shàngbian	1-6
上等	（形）	shàngděng	6-7
上课	（动）	shàngkè	2-2
上面	（名）	shàngmiàn	4-2
上网	（动）	shàngwǎng	3-10
上午	（名）	shàngwǔ	2-2
上衣	（名）	shàngyī	3-9
上涨	（动）	shàngzhǎng	6-3
稍	（副）	shāo	4-6
少	（形）	shǎo	2-2
蛇	（名）	shé	4-5
设备	（名）	shèbèi	6-6
设计	（动、名）	shèjì	4-5
社会	（名）	shèhuì	5-2
摄氏度	（量）	shèshìdù	3-2
谁	（代）	shéi	2-1
伸	（动）	shēn	6-2
身材	（名）	shēncái	6-3
身高	（名）	shēngāo	5-1
身上	（名）	shēnshang	3-9
身体	（名）	shēntǐ	1-7
深	（形）	shēn	6-2
深厚	（形）	shēnhòu	3-10
深情	（形、名）	shēnqíng	6-4
什么	（代）	shénme	1-4
神经病	（名）	shénjīngbìng	6-9
神圣	（形）	shénshèng	2-5
婶子	（名）	shěnzi	4-7

升	（动）	shēng	5-4	实践	（动）	shíjiàn	6-9
生	（动）	shēng	4-9	实时	（副）	shíshí	6-10
生病	（动）	shēngbìng	4-9	实现	（动）	shíxiàn	4-3
生产	（动）	shēngchǎn	3-9	实在	（副、形）	shízài	4-2
生词	（名）	shēngcí	1-5	食		shí	4-5
生动	（形）	shēngdòng	5-6	食品	（名）	shípǐn	4-3
生分	（形）	shēngfen	6-5	食堂	（名）	shítáng	1-6
生活	（名）	shēnghuó	2-10	使	（动）	shǐ	3-6
生气	（动）	shēngqì	4-4	使用	（动）	shǐyòng	5-10
生日	（名）	shēngrì	2-6	世代	（名）	shìdài	6-9
生意	（名）	shēngyi	3-2	世界	（名）	shìjiè	2-2
生鱼片	（名）	shēngyúpiàn	4-6	世上	（名）	shìshàng	3-10
声	（名）	shēng	5-6	世世代代		shìshìdàidài	6-9
声调	（名）	shēngdiào	1-10	市	（名）	shì	2-10
声音	（名）	shēngyīn	5-6	市场	（名）	shìchǎng	3-3
省	（动）	shěng	5-2	市区	（名）	shìqū	2-10
省	（名）	shěng	5-5	似的	（助）	shìde	5-6
失眠	（动）	shīmián	6-9	事情	（名）	shìqing	3-8
失望	（形）	shīwàng	5-1	事儿	（名）	shìr	1-9
失业	（动）	shīyè	6-3	事实	（名）	shìshí	5-10
师傅	（名）	shīfu	3-9	试	（动）	shì	1-10
诗	（名）	shī	4-1	视频	（名）	shìpín	3-10
诗人	（名）	shīrén	4-1	是	（动）	shì	1-3
十	（数）	shí	1-1	适合	（动）	shìhé	5-6
十分	（副）	shífēn	3-9	室		shì	2-4
十字路口		shízì lùkǒu	4-9	收	（动）	shōu	3-6
石（头）	（名）	shí(tou)	5-5	收获	（名）	shōuhuò	6-10
石雕	（名）	shídiāo	6-8	收件人	（名）	shōujiànrén	5-9
石窟	（名）	shíkū	6-8	收据	（名）	shōujù	3-5
时代	（名）	shídài	6-5	收入	（名）	shōurù	6-8
时光	（名）	shíguāng	3-10	收拾	（动）	shōushi	2-6
时候	（名）	shíhou	1-10	收听	（动）	shōutīng	6-10
时间	（名）	shíjiān	2-4	手	（名）	shǒu	1-6
时髦	（形）	shímáo	6-2	手表	（名）	shǒubiǎo	1-6
时期	（名）	shíqī	5-5	手机	（名）	shǒujī	1-6

手术	（名）	shǒushù	4-10
手提电脑		shǒutí diànnǎo	3-10
手续	（名）	shǒuxù	6-9
手纸	（名）	shǒuzhǐ	5-10
手指	（名）	shǒuzhǐ	6-4
首	（量）	shǒu	3-10
首		shǒu	6-3
首都	（名）	shǒudū	6-3
首先	（副）	shǒuxiān	5-6
寿		shòu	2-7
受	（动）	shòu	3-9
受伤	（动）	shòushāng	5-10
售货员	（名）	shòuhuòyuán	3-9
售票员	（名）	shòupiàoyuán	5-1
瘦	（形）	shòu	5-3
书	（名）	shū	1-6
书包	（名）	shūbāo	5-8
书店	（名）	shūdiàn	1-6
书法	（名）	shūfǎ	4-1
书房	（名）	shūfáng	4-7
书柜	（名）	shūguì	3-7
书架	（名）	shūjià	1-6
书桌	（名）	shūzhuō	3-7
叔叔	（名）	shūshu	4-4
舒服	（形）	shūfu	2-9
输	（动）	shū	4-1
蔬菜	（名）	shūcài	6-6
熟	（形）	shú	4-2
属	（动）	shǔ	2-6
数	（动）	shǔ	2-7
树	（名）	shù	4-10
树林	（名）	shùlín	4-10
数		shù	2-7
数码相机	（名）	shùmǎ xiàngjī	5-8
数目	（名）	shùmù	6-6

数学	（名）	shùxué	4-8
数字	（名）	shùzì	2-7
刷卡	（动）	shuākǎ	4-6
摔	（动）	shuāi	5-8
帅	（形）	shuài	5-1
双	（形）	shuāng	2-3
水	（名）	shuǐ	2-8
水果	（名）	shuǐguǒ	2-6
水面	（名）	shuǐmiàn	6-7
水平	（名）	shuǐpíng	3-5
水煮牛肉		shuǐzhǔ niúròu	4-5
税	（名）	shuì	6-10
睡觉	（动）	shuìjiào	3-1
顺	（介）	shùn	4-9
顺	（动）	shùn	6-2
顺便	（副）	shùnbiàn	2-10
顺利	（形）	shùnlì	2-7
顺路	（形）	shùnlù	6-2
说	（动）	shuō	1-5
说不定	（副）	shuōbudìng	4-4
说法	（名）	shuōfǎ	5-5
说明	（动）	shuōmíng	6-4
硕士	（名）	shuòshì	5-6
司机	（名）	sījī	5-1
丝	（名）	sī	4-6
丝绸	（名）	sīchóu	3-9
私人	（名）	sīrén	3-8
私事	（名）	sīshì	5-2
死	（动）	sǐ	5-7
四	（数）	sì	1-1
四合院儿	（名）	sìhéyuànr	4-7
四世同堂		sì shì tóngtáng	4-7
似	（动）	sì	6-6
送	（动）	sòng	2-2
酥油	（名）	sūyóu	6-7

酥油茶	（名）	sūyóuchá	6-7
俗话	（名）	súhuà	4-2
速成	（动）	sùchéng	1-8
宿舍	（名）	sùshè	1-7
酸	（形）	suān	4-6
酸辣汤	（名）	suānlàtāng	4-6
算是	（动）	suànshì	4-8
虽然	（连）	suīrán	3-10
随	（动）	suí	6-3
随便	（动）	suíbiàn	2-9
随时	（副）	suíshí	5-2
岁	（量）	suì	2-9
岁数	（名）	suìshu	4-7
孙子	（名）	sūnzi	6-10
所	（量）	suǒ	3-6
所	（名）	suǒ	5-1
所以	（连）	suǒyǐ	5-3
所有	（形）	suǒyǒu	4-4
所长	（名）	suǒzhǎng	5-1
		T	
他	（代）	tā	1-2
她	（代）	tā	1-2
塔	（名）	tǎ	6-3
台	（量）	tái	3-8
台阶	（名）	táijiē	5-5
抬	（动）	tái	5-7
太	（副）	tài	1-4
太极拳	（名）	tàijíquán	3-10
太太	（名）	tàitai	3-9
太阳	（名）	tàiyáng	5-4
态度	（名）	tàidu	3-9
谈	（动）	tán	2-1
弹	（动）	tán	6-8
坦率	（形）	tǎnshuài	6-10

汤	（名）	tāng	4-6
糖	（名）	táng	4-4
躺	（动）	tǎng	4-7
趟	（量）	tàng	5-8
掏	（动）	tāo	6-2
讨	（动）	tǎo	5-1
讨价还价		tǎojià-huánjià	3-9
讨论	（动）	tǎolùn	6-5
讨厌	（动）	tǎoyàn	6-4
套	（量）	tào	3-3
特别	（副）	tèbié	2-5
特色	（名）	tèsè	4-1
特意	（副）	tèyì	5-9
疼	（形）	téng	2-9
腾飞	（动）	téngfēi	5-5
踢	（动）	tī	3-1
提	（动）	tí	3-7
提高	（动）	tígāo	3-10
提前	（动）	tíqián	5-6
提醒	（动）	tíxǐng	6-9
题目	（名）	tímù	6-1
体温	（名）	tǐwēn	2-9
体育	（名）	tǐyù	3-1
体育场	（名）	tǐyùchǎng	3-1
体重	（名）	tǐzhòng	4-4
天	（名）	tiān	1-5
天空	（名）	tiānkōng	5-4
天气	（名）	tiānqì	2-10
天使	（名）	tiānshǐ	4-10
添	（动）	tiān	4-9
甜	（形）	tián	4-4
填	（动）	tián	3-8
填写	（动）	tiánxiě	5-9
挑	（动）	tiāo	3-9
条	（量）	tiáo	2-8

条件	（名）	tiáojiàn	3-10
调	（动）	tiáo	6-9
跳舞	（动）	tiàowǔ	3-3
贴	（动）	tiē	3-5
铁路	（名）	tiělù	4-4
厅	（名）	tīng	3-6
听	（动）	tīng	1-10
听	（名）	tīng	4-6
听力	（名）	tīnglì	2-4
听说	（动）	tīngshuō	2-8
听写	（动）	tīngxiě	1-10
停	（动）	tíng	5-3
挺	（副）	tǐng	4-1
通	（动）	tōng	2-9
……通		…tōng	3-5
通过	（介）	tōngguò	6-10
通知	（名、动）	tōngzhī	2-6
同	（副）	tóng	2-10
同居	（动）	tóngjū	2-10
同时	（名、连）	tóngshí	6-5
同学	（名）	tóngxué	1-8
同样	（形）	tóngyàng	6-2
同意	（动）	tóngyì	3-6
统计	（动）	tǒngjì	5-6
统一	（动）	tǒngyī	5-5
痛	（形）	tòng	6-4
痛苦	（形）	tòngkǔ	5-10
痛快	（形）	tòngkuai	6-9
偷	（动、副）	tōu	4-4
偷偷	（副）	tōutōu	4-4
头	（名）	tóu	2-9
头发	（名）	tóufa	6-3
透	（形）	tòu	5-9
突然	（形）	tūrán	2-10

图	（名）	tú	1-7
图片	（名）	túpiàn	5-5
图书馆	（名）	túshūguǎn	1-7
兔	（名）	tù	2-6
兔子	（名）	tùzi	2-6
团圆	（动）	tuányuán	5-4
推	（动）	tuī	4-8
腿	（名）	tuǐ	5-8
退	（动）	tuì	5-3
拖拉	（形）	tuōlā	6-9
脱	（动）	tuō	6-4

W

娃娃菜	（名）	wáwacài	4-6
袜子	（名）	wàzi	3-6
外	（名）	wài	2-8
外币	（名）	wàibì	3-8
外边	（名）	wàibian	2-8
外国	（名）	wàiguó	3-6
外科	（名）	wàikē	4-10
外面	（名）	wàimiàn	4-2
外人	（名）	wàirén	6-9
外套	（名）	wàitào	3-9
外文	（名）	wàiwén	1-8
外语	（名）	wàiyǔ	1-8
弯	（形）	wān	6-3
弯曲	（形）	wānqū	5-5
丸	（名、量）	wán	3-4
丸药	（名）	wányào	3-4
完	（动）	wán	2-5
完成	（动）	wánchéng	3-7
完好	（形）	wánhǎo	6-8
完全	（副）	wánquán	1-10
玩儿	（动）	wánr	1-8
玩笑	（名）	wánxiào	3-6

晚	（形）	wǎn	3-7
晚报	（名）	wǎnbào	4-2
晚饭	（名）	wǎnfàn	3-1
晚会	（名）	wǎnhuì	2-6
晚上	（名）	wǎnshang	1-5
碗	（名）	wǎn	4-6
万	（数）	wàn	2-7
万事	（名）	wànshì	2-7
万事如意		wànshì-rúyì	2-7
万一	（连）	wànyī	6-10
网	（名）	wǎng	3-3
网吧	（名）	wǎngbā	3-10
网购	（动）	wǎnggòu	3-3
网络	（名）	wǎngluò	6-6
网球	（名）	wǎngqiú	4-5
往	（介）	wǎng	3-5
往常	（名）	wǎngcháng	6-10
往往	（副）	wǎngwǎng	6-5
忘	（动）	wàng	3-6
忘记	（动）	wàngjì	3-6
望	（动）	wàng	5-4
危险	（形）	wēixiǎn	6-9
微	（形）	wēi	3-10
微风	（名）	wēifēng	3-10
微笑	（动、名）	wēixiào	6-2
微信	（名）	wēixìn	3-3
为	（动）	wéi	6-8
为人	（名）	wéirén	6-10
围	（动）	wéi	5-5
围绕	（动）	wéirào	5-5
维生素	（名）	wéishēngsù	6-7
伟大	（形）	wěidà	5-5
伪劣	（形）	wěiliè	4-4
尾号	（名）	wěihào	6-10

卫生	（名、形）	wèishēng	5-10
卫生纸	（名）	wèishēngzhǐ	5-10
为	（介）	wèi	2-1
为了	（介）	wèile	4-4
为什么		wèi shénme	2-1
位	（量）	wèi	1-8
味道	（名）	wèidao	3-3
味儿	（名）	wèir	5-1
胃	（名）	wèi	4-10
喂	（叹）	wèi	3-1
文化	（名）	wénhuà	2-5
文件	（名）	wénjiàn	3-8
文学	（名）	wénxué	3-5
文艺	（名）	wényì	6-9
文章	（名）	wénzhāng	2-6
闻名	（动）	wénmíng	4-5
吻	（动）	wěn	6-10
问	（动）	wèn	1-8
问好	（动）	wènhǎo	5-3
问号	（名）	wènhào	5-5
问候	（动）	wènhòu	3-10
问题	（名）	wèntí	2-5
我	（代）	wǒ	1-2
卧	（动）	wò	6-8
卧室	（名）	wòshì	4-4
握	（动）	wò	3-5
乌龙茶	（名）	wūlóngchá	2-9
屋	（名）	wū	3-7
屋子	（名）	wūzi	3-7
无	（动）	wú	6-4
无轨电车		wúguǐ-diànchē	4-4
无话不说		wúhuà-bùshuō	6-10
无价	（动）	wújià	6-4
无论如何		wúlùn-rúhé	6-3

无忧无虑		wúyōu-wúlǜ	6-10
五	（数）	wǔ	1-1
五花八门		wǔhuā-bāmén	6-6
午饭	（名）	wǔfàn	3-1
捂	（动）	wǔ	5-8
勿	（副）	wù	6-4
物价	（名）	wùjià	6-3
物理	（名）	wùlǐ	4-8
误会	（动）	wùhuì	2-10
		X	
西	（名）	xī	3-1
西餐	（名）	xīcān	3-5
西方	（名）	xīfāng	3-6
西服	（名）	xīfú	3-9
西瓜	（名）	xīgua	2-9
西面	（名）	xīmiàn	4-2
西药	（名）	xīyào	3-4
吸	（动）	xī	4-4
希望	（动）	xīwàng	3-7
稀		xī	4-2
习惯	（动）	xíguàn	2-10
媳妇	（名）	xífu	5-7
洗	（动）	xǐ	2-6
洗衣店	（名）	xǐyīdiàn	3-3
洗澡	（动）	xǐzǎo	3-10
喜	（形）	xǐ	4-4
喜爱	（动）	xǐ'ài	6-10
喜欢	（动）	xǐhuan	2-3
喜糖	（名）	xǐtáng	4-4
戏	（名）	xì	5-7
系	（名）	xì	2-2
系统	（形、名）	xìtǒng	4-1
细	（形）	xì	6-6
下	（动）	xià	1-7
下	（名）	xià	2-8
下班	（动）	xiàbān	2-10
下边	（名）	xiàbian	2-8
下课	（动）	xiàkè	1-7
下面	（名）	xiàmiàn	4-2
下午	（名）	xiàwǔ	2-2
下载	（动）	xiàzài	6-2
夏季	（名）	xiàjì	2-3
夏天	（名）	xiàtiān	2-3
先	（副）	xiān	3-6
先生	（名）	xiānsheng	2-3
鲜	（形）	xiān	4-10
鲜花	（名）	xiānhuā	4-10
咸	（形）	xián	6-1
显得	（动）	xiǎnde	6-2
现代	（形）	xiàndài	4-1
现金	（名）	xiànjīn	2-3
现在	（名）	xiànzài	2-2
线	（名）	xiàn	5-6
馅儿	（名）	xiànr	6-1
乡	（名）	xiāng	6-4
相	（副）	xiāng	3-10
相处	（动）	xiāngchǔ	6-9
相当	（副）	xiāngdāng	3-9
相亲相爱		xiāngqīn-xiāng'ài	3-10
相同	（形）	xiāngtóng	6-1
相信	（动）	xiāngxìn	4-8
香	（形）	xiāng	4-6
香蕉	（名）	xiāngjiāo	5-3
箱子	（名）	xiāngzi	5-7
享福	（动）	xiǎngfú	5-7
享受	（动）	xiǎngshòu	6-7
想	（动）	xiǎng	1-9
想法	（名）	xiǎngfa	6-1

向	（介）	xiàng	3-7
相	（名）	xiàng	2-9
相片儿	（名）	xiàngpiānr	5-6
向导	（名）	xiàngdǎo	6-8
项链	（名）	xiàngliàn	5-9
项目	（名）	xiàngmù	6-6
巷	（名）	xiàng	6-6
象棋	（名）	xiàngqí	5-7
象征	（名）	xiàngzhēng	5-4
像	（动）	xiàng	3-6
消化	（动）	xiāohuà	6-7
消失	（动）	xiāoshī	6-2
消息	（名）	xiāoxi	6-1
小	（形）	xiǎo	1-9
小便	（动、名）	xiǎobiàn	3-4
小吃	（名）	xiǎochī	4-5
小伙子	（名）	xiǎohuǒzi	5-1
小姐	（名）	xiǎojiě	2-4
小康	（形）	xiǎokāng	6-5
小时	（名）	xiǎoshí	2-4
小说	（名）	xiǎoshuō	3-3
小偷儿	（名）	xiǎotōur	5-8
小心	（动）	xiǎoxīn	4-9
小学	（名）	xiǎoxué	2-1
孝顺	（动）	xiàoshùn	5-7
孝心	（名）	xiàoxīn	5-7
校	（名）	xiào	2-1
校园	（名）	xiàoyuán	1-7
校长	（名）	xiàozhǎng	2-1
笑	（动）	xiào	2-9
笑话	（动、名）	xiàohua	5-10
效果	（名）	xiàoguǒ	6-4
些	（量）	xiē	2-8
鞋	（名）	xié	3-3

写	（动）	xiě	1-5
血	（名）	xiě	3-4
泻	（动）	xiè	4-10
谢	（动）	xiè	1-5
心	（名）	xīn	2-7
心爱	（形）	xīn'ài	5-9
心烦	（形）	xīnfán	6-9
心里	（名）	xīnli	6-9
心情	（名）	xīnqíng	6-9
心事	（名）	xīnshì	6-9
心思	（名）	xīnsi	5-8
心想事成		xīnxiǎng-shìchéng	2-7
辛苦	（形）	xīnkǔ	6-4
辛劳	（形）	xīnláo	6-10
新	（形）	xīn	2-7
新郎	（名）	xīnláng	6-10
新年	（名）	xīnnián	2-7
新娘	（名）	xīnniáng	6-10
新奇	（形）	xīnqí	5-2
新闻	（名）	xīnwén	4-1
新鲜	（形）	xīnxian	6-6
信	（名）	xìn	2-1
信	（动）	xìn	4-8
信封	（名）	xìnfēng	5-7
信息	（名）	xìnxī	6-7
信用卡	（名）	xìnyòngkǎ	5-9
信誉	（名）	xìnyù	5-3
信纸	（名）	xìnzhǐ	5-10
兴奋	（形）	xīngfèn	5-6
星级	（名）	xīngjí	5-7
星期	（名）	xīngqī	2-10
星期日	（名）	xīngqīrì	2-10
星期天	（名）	xīngqītiān	2-10
星星	（名）	xīngxing	5-4

行	（形）	xíng	1-7
行动	（动）	xíngdòng	6-1
行李	（名）	xíngli	4-7
行政区	（名）	xíngzhèngqū	5-5
形	（名）	xíng	6-1
形状	（名）	xíngzhuàng	6-1
醒	（动）	xǐng	5-9
兴趣	（名）	xìngqù	2-5
幸福	（形）	xìngfú	2-7
幸亏	（副）	xìngkuī	6-9
……性		…xìng	4-10
姓	（名、动）	xìng	1-3
休息	（动）	xiūxi	1-7
修	（动）	xiū	2-9
修建	（动）	xiūjiàn	5-5
修理	（动）	xiūlǐ	2-9
秀气	（形）	xiùqi	6-3
绣	（动）	xiù	6-4
需要	（动、名）	xūyào	5-10
许	（动）	xǔ	4-5
许多	（数）	xǔduō	4-3
宣传	（动）	xuānchuán	6-10
宣传语	（名）	xuānchuányǔ	6-10
选择	（动）	xuǎnzé	6-1
学	（动）	xué	1-7
学生	（名）	xuésheng	1-8
学术	（名）	xuéshù	5-6
学问	（名）	xuéwen	4-5
学习	（动）	xuéxí	1-7
学校	（名）	xuéxiào	1-8
学院	（名）	xuéyuàn	1-8
雪	（名）	xuě	3-2
雪碧	（名）	xuěbì	4-6
血压	（名）	xuèyā	3-4
训练	（动）	xùnliàn	3-7
驯	（动）	xùn	5-8
Y			
鸭	（名）	yā	4-3
牙	（名）	yá	2-9
牙齿	（名）	yáchǐ	6-3
轧	（动）	yà	6-4
呀	（助）	ya	2-2
烟	（名）	yān	4-4
严	（形）	yán	4-8
严格	（形）	yángé	3-7
沿	（介）	yán	4-3
研究	（动）	yánjiū	2-1
研究生	（名）	yánjiūshēng	2-1
颜色	（名）	yánsè	3-9
眼	（名）	yǎn	4-1
眼睛	（名）	yǎnjing	4-1
眼镜	（名）	yǎnjìng	5-2
眼前	（名）	yǎnqián	4-1
演	（动）	yǎn	5-7
演出	（动）	yǎnchū	5-7
演员	（名）	yǎnyuán	6-5
宴会	（名）	yànhuì	6-8
羊	（名）	yáng	5-3
阳台	（名）	yángtái	6-3
养	（动）	yǎng	5-7
养成		yǎngchéng	5-10
样	（量）	yàng	5-9
样儿	（名）	yàngr	2-3
样子	（名）	yàngzi	3-9
要求	（名）	yāoqiú	3-7
邀请	（动）	yāoqǐng	4-2
遥远	（形）	yáoyuǎn	3-10

药	（名）	yào	2-9
药方	（名）	yàofāng	3-4
药膏	（名）	yàogāo	6-4
药片儿	（名）	yàopiànr	3-4
要	（能动）	yào	1-7
要	（连）	yào	2-5
要紧	（形）	yàojǐn	3-4
要命	（动）	yàomìng	4-9
要是	（连）	yàoshi	2-5
要死	（动）	yàosǐ	4-9
钥匙	（名）	yàoshi	4-9
爷爷	（名）	yéye	1-9
也	（副）	yě	1-4
野	（形）	yě	5-8
页	（量）	yè	3-5
夜	（名）	yè	3-4
夜间	（名）	yèjiān	3-2
夜里	（名）	yèli	3-4
夜晚	（名）	yèwǎn	5-4
一	（数）	yī	1-1
一……就……		yī…jiù…	3-4
一……也/都……		yī…yě/dōu…	5-6
衣服	（名）	yīfu	2-3
衣柜	（名）	yīguì	3-7
医生	（名）	yīshēng	6-4
医学	（名）	yīxué	6-7
医院	（名）	yīyuàn	2-1
一半儿	（数）	yíbànr	3-4
一定	（副）	yídìng	1-10
一共	（副）	yígòng	1-4
一会儿	（数量）	yíhuìr	3-8
一块儿	（副）	yíkuàir	4-5
一律	（副）	yílǜ	5-3

一切	（代）	yíqiè	2-7
一下儿	（数量）	yíxiàr	1-8
一下子	（副）	yíxiàzi	6-5
一样	（形）	yíyàng	1-10
一致	（副）	yízhì	6-5
姨	（名）	yí	4-7
姨父	（名）	yífu	4-7
遗产	（名）	yíchǎn	5-5
遗憾	（形）	yíhàn	2-7
已	（副）	yǐ	2-6
已经	（副）	yǐjīng	2-6
以	（介）	yǐ	6-6
以后	（名）	yǐhòu	1-8
以前	（名）	yǐqián	3-1
以上	（名）	yǐshàng	2-3
以为	（动）	yǐwéi	4-4
以下	（名）	yǐxià	2-3
椅子	（名）	yǐzi	3-7
一般	（形）	yìbān	4-8
一边……一边……		yìbiān…yìbiān…	1-10
一点儿	（数量）	yìdiǎnr	2-3
一回生，两回熟		yì huí shēng, liǎng huí shú	4-2
一连	（副）	yìlián	6-9
一起	（副）	yìqǐ	1-9
一生	（名）	yìshēng	3-5
一时	（副）	yìshí	5-4
一手儿	（名）	yìshǒur	4-8
一些	（数量）	yìxiē	2-8
一衣带水		yìyīdàishuǐ	6-9
一直	（副）	yìzhí	4-2
亿	（数）	yì	3-2
义务	（形）	yìwù	5-1
艺术	（名）	yìshù	6-5

意见	（名）	yìjiàn	3-7
意思	（名）	yìsi	1-10
因此	（连）	yīncǐ	4-9
因为	（连）	yīnwei	3-4
阴	（形）	yīn	3-2
音节	（名）	yīnjié	6-5
音频	（名）	yīnpín	3-10
音译	（动）	yīnyì	6-7
音乐	（名）	yīnyuè	2-6
银	（名）	yín	3-10
银白	（形）	yínbái	5-4
银行	（名）	yínháng	3-8
银婚	（名）	yínhūn	3-10
银子	（名）	yínzi	3-10
引起	（动）	yǐnqǐ	6-6
饮茶	（动）	yǐnchá	6-7
饮料	（名）	yǐnliào	2-9
印象	（名）	yìnxiàng	6-2
应该	（能动）	yīnggāi	3-5
营业	（动）	yíngyè	2-2
营业员	（名）	yíngyèyuán	2-2
赢	（动）	yíng	4-1
赢得	（动）	yíngdé	4-1
影响	（动、名）	yǐngxiǎng	4-4
硬	（形）	yìng	6-7
硬币	（名）	yìngbì	6-7
哟	（叹）	yō	2-9
拥挤	（形）	yōngjǐ	5-6
永远	（副）	yǒngyuǎn	2-7
用	（动）	yòng	1-10
用功	（形）	yònggōng	3-4
优惠	（形）	yōuhuì	2-3
优良	（形）	yōuliáng	5-1
优美	（形）	yōuměi	4-10

优盘	（名）	yōupán	3-4
优秀	（形）	yōuxiù	5-1
悠久	（形）	yōujiǔ	4-1
由	（介）	yóu	4-1
由于	（介、连）	yóuyú	6-6
邮费	（名）	yóufèi	3-5
邮件	（名）	yóujiàn	2-1
邮局	（名）	yóujú	3-5
邮票	（名）	yóupiào	3-5
油	（名）	yóu	5-10
油腻	（形）	yóunì	4-5
油条	（名）	yóutiáo	6-1
游	（动）	yóu	4-3
游览	（动）	yóulǎn	4-3
游泳	（动）	yóuyǒng	3-2
友好	（形）	yǒuhǎo	6-9
友谊	（名）	yǒuyì	3-1
有	（动）	yǒu	1-5
有的	（代）	yǒude	4-8
有点儿	（副）	yǒudiǎnr	2-10
有关	（介、动）	yǒuguān	6-6
有害	（形）	yǒuhài	4-4
有名	（形）	yǒumíng	4-3
有时	（副）	yǒushí	3-7
有时候	（副）	yǒushíhou	3-7
有些	（代）	yǒuxiē	5-2
有意思		yǒu yìsi	2-5
有用	（形）	yǒuyòng	3-3
又	（副）	yòu	2-4
又……又……		yòu…yòu…	3-3
右	（名）	yòu	2-8
右边	（名）	yòubian	2-8
右面	（名）	yòumiàn	4-2
幼儿	（名）	yòu'ér	2-10

幼儿园	（名）	yòu'éryuán	2-10
于	（介）	yú	6-7
于是	（连）	yúshì	3-9
鱼香肉丝		yúxiāng ròusī	4-6
愉快	（形）	yúkuài	5-6
宇航员	（名）	yǔhángyuán	5-5
羽毛球	（名）	yǔmáoqiú	4-5
雨	（名）	yǔ	3-2
语伴儿	（名）	yǔbànr	3-8
语调	（名）	yǔdiào	5-10
语法	（名）	yǔfǎ	2-4
语文	（名）	yǔwén	6-5
语音	（名）	yǔyīn	1-10
预报	（名）	yùbào	3-2
预订	（动）	yùdìng	2-3
预习	（动）	yùxí	1-7
遇	（动）	yù	1-7
遇到		yùdào	2-10
遇见	（动）	yùjiàn	1-7
元	（量）	yuán	2-3
元宵	（名）	yuánxiāo	5-4
……员		…yuán	3-9
原来	（副）	yuánlái	4-1
原谅	（动）	yuánliàng	6-9
原因	（名）	yuányīn	2-5
圆	（形）	yuán	5-4
圆珠笔	（名）	yuánzhūbǐ	2-2
远	（形）	yuǎn	1-9
远在天边，近在眼前		yuǎn zài tiānbiān, jìn zài yǎnqián	4-1
院	（名）	yuàn	4-1
院长	（名）	yuànzhǎng	2-1
院子	（名）	yuànzi	4-7
愿	（能动）	yuàn	3-10

愿望	（名）	yuànwàng	4-3
愿意	（能动）	yuànyì	3-3
约	（动）	yuē	5-9
约	（副）	yuē	6-8
约会	（名）	yuēhuì	5-9
月	（名）	yuè	3-2
月饼	（名）	yuèbing	5-3
月光	（名）	yuèguāng	5-4
月亮	（名）	yuèliang	5-4
阅读	（动）	yuèdú	3-8
阅览室	（名）	yuèlǎnshì	3-3
越……越……		yuè…yuè…	5-8
越来越……		yuè lái yuè…	6-6
云	（名）	yún	3-2
云彩	（名）	yúncai	5-4
允许	（动）	yǔnxǔ	4-5
运	（动）	yùn	3-5
运动	（名）	yùndòng	4-5
运动员	（名）	yùndòngyuán	4-9
Z			
杂技	（名）	zájì	5-3
杂志	（名）	zázhì	3-5
仔细	（形）	zǐxì	6-8
再	（副）	zài	1-7
再见	（动）	zàijiàn	1-7
再说	（连）	zàishuō	5-3
在	（动）	zài	1-5
在	（副）	zài	4-1
咱们	（代）	zánmen	3-1
攒	（动）	zǎn	5-7
赞扬	（动）	zànyáng	4-1
脏	（形）	zāng	6-6
糟糕	（形）	zāogāo	2-6

早	（形）	zǎo	2-9
早茶	（名）	zǎochá	6-1
早晨	（名）	zǎochen	5-9
早出晚归		zǎochū-wǎnguī	6-10
早饭	（名）	zǎofàn	3-1
早日	（副）	zǎorì	2-9
早上	（名）	zǎoshang	3-1
造句	（动）	zàojù	1-10
责怪	（动）	zéguài	5-10
怎么	（代）	zěnme	1-10
怎么回事		zěnme huí shì	3-8
怎么样	（代）	zěnmeyàng	1-7
增加	（动）	zēngjiā	4-4
增长	（动）	zēngzhǎng	4-5
炸	（动）	zhá	6-1
炸糕	（名）	zhágāo	6-1
窄	（形）	zhǎi	6-6
展览	（动）	zhǎnlǎn	5-7
战场	（名）	zhànchǎng	5-8
战争	（名）	zhànzhēng	5-8
站	（动）	zhàn	4-7
站	（名）	zhàn	4-9
张	（量）	zhāng	2-2
长	（动）	zhǎng	4-1
涨	（动）	zhǎng	6-3
掌握	（动）	zhǎngwò	5-10
丈夫	（名）	zhàngfu	3-6
账	（名）	zhàng	4-6
招待	（动）	zhāodài	6-1
招待会	（名）	zhāodàihuì	6-1
招呼	（动）	zhāohu	5-3
招生	（动）	zhāoshēng	4-1
招手	（动）	zhāoshǒu	6-2
着	（动）	zháo	3-4
着急	（形）	zháojí	1-6
找	（动）	zhǎo	1-6
召开	（动）	zhàokāi	6-4
照	（动）	zhào	2-9
照顾	（动）	zhàogù	3-9
照片	（名）	zhàopiàn	3-6
照相	（动）	zhàoxiàng	2-9
照相机	（名）	zhàoxiàngjī	5-8
哲学	（名）	zhéxué	5-7
这	（代）	zhè	1-4
这边	（名）	zhèbian	1-5
这里	（代）	zhèli	3-10
这儿	（代）	zhèr	1-6
这些	（代）	zhèxiē	3-3
着	（助）	zhe	3-5
着呢	（助）	zhene	6-3
珍贵	（形）	zhēnguì	5-9
珍惜	（动）	zhēnxī	4-2
真	（副）	zhēn	2-4
真	（形）	zhēn	2-10
真诚	（形）	zhēnchéng	6-10
真情	（名）	zhēnqíng	6-10
真实	（形）	zhēnshí	5-10
真正	（形）	zhēnzhèng	5-5
阵	（量）	zhèn	3-10
镇	（名）	zhèn	6-3
争取	（动）	zhēngqǔ	4-2
征求	（动）	zhēngqiú	6-5
整个	（形）	zhěnggè	5-6
整齐	（形）	zhěngqí	2-6
正	（副）	zhèng	1-10
正	（形）	zhèng	6-6
正常	（形）	zhèngcháng	2-9
正好	（副、形）	zhènghǎo	4-5

正巧	（副）	zhèngqiǎo	6-4
正确	（形）	zhèngquè	5-10
正在	（副）	zhèngzài	2-6
证书	（名）	zhèngshū	4-2
政府	（名）	zhèngfǔ	4-5
挣	（动）	zhèng	5-2
……之一		zhī yī	4-5
支	（量）	zhī	2-2
支撑	（动）	zhīchēng	6-10
只	（量）	zhī	2-1
枝	（量）	zhī	2-7
知	（动）	zhī	2-2
知道	（动）	zhīdao	2-2
知识	（名）	zhīshi	5-8
直	（副）	zhí	6-2
值得	（动）	zhíde	3-6
职业	（名）	zhíyè	2-5
职员	（名）	zhíyuán	2-1
止	（动）	zhǐ	4-10
止痛膏	（名）	zhǐtònggāo	6-4
只	（副）	zhǐ	1-9
只好	（副）	zhǐhǎo	5-3
只是	（副）	zhǐshì	2-5
只是	（连）	zhǐshì	3-7
只要……就……		zhǐyào…jiù…	3-5
只有	（连）	zhǐyǒu	3-10
纸	（名）	zhǐ	3-8
指	（动）	zhǐ	6-3
至	（动）	zhì	6-5
至今	（副）	zhìjīn	6-5
质量	（名）	zhìliàng	3-9
治	（动）	zhì	4-6
治疗	（动）	zhìliáo	4-10

中	（形）	zhōng	3-2
中	（名）	zhōng	4-2
中餐	（名）	zhōngcān	3-5
中间	（名）	zhōngjiān	2-9
中午	（名）	zhōngwǔ	3-1
中学	（名）	zhōngxué	2-1
中药	（名）	zhōngyào	3-4
终于	（副）	zhōngyú	5-5
钟	（名）	zhōng	3-1
钟头	（名）	zhōngtóu	5-2
衷心	（形）	zhōngxīn	6-4
种	（量）	zhǒng	2-2
种类	（名）	zhǒnglèi	6-1
种	（动）	zhòng	4-9
种植	（动）	zhòngzhí	6-7
重	（形）	zhòng	3-5
重量	（名）	zhòngliàng	3-5
重视	（动）	zhòngshì	6-5
重要	（形）	zhòngyào	4-8
周	（名）	zhōu	2-3
周	（量）	zhōu	5-5
周到	（形）	zhōudào	3-6
周岁	（名）	zhōusuì	6-5
周围	（名）	zhōuwéi	4-4
猪	（名）	zhū	4-5
猪手	（名）	zhūshǒu	4-5
主意	（名）	< 口 >zhúyi	2-4
主持	（动）	zhǔchí	6-6
主持人	（名）	zhǔchírén	6-6
主妇	（名）	zhǔfù	2-1
主讲	（动）	zhǔjiǎng	4-1
主人	（名）	zhǔrén	5-7
主任	（名）	zhǔrèn	2-1
主食	（名）	zhǔshí	4-6

主席	（名）	zhǔxí	3-9
主席台	（名）	zhǔxítái	3-9
主要	（形）	zhǔyào	5-4
煮	（动）	zhǔ	5-7
嘱咐	（动）	zhǔfu	6-4
住	（动）	zhù	1-8
住院	（动）	zhùyuàn	4-9
住址	（名）	zhùzhǐ	2-10
注册	（动）	zhùcè	6-2
注意	（动）	zhùyì	1-7
祝	（动）	zhù	2-7
祝福	（动）	zhùfú	6-10
祝贺	（动）	zhùhè	4-7
著名	（形）	zhùmíng	6-3
抓紧	（动）	zhuājǐn	4-2
专家	（名）	zhuānjiā	6-7
专门	（副、形）	zhuānmén	3-5
专心	（形）	zhuānxīn	3-6
砖	（名）	zhuān	5-5
转	（动）	zhuǎn	3-2
转	（动）	zhuàn	4-4
赚	（动）	zhuàn	6-10
装	（动）	zhuāng	5-3
壮	（形）	zhuàng	5-8
状况	（名）	zhuàngkuàng	5-6
撞	（动）	zhuàng	6-10
准	（形）	zhǔn	2-10
准备	（动）	zhǔnbèi	2-5
准确	（形）	zhǔnquè	5-9
准时	（形）	zhǔnshí	2-10
桌	（量）	zhuō	5-7
桌子	（名）	zhuōzi	1-6
滋味	（名）	zīwèi	5-6
子		zǐ	4-8
紫	（形）	zǐ	1-9
自	（介）	zì	6-5
自从	（介）	zìcóng	6-5
自己	（代）	zìjǐ	2-9
自来水	（名）	zìláishuǐ	6-7
自然	（名、形）	zìrán	6-8
自我	（代）	zìwǒ	6-4
自行车	（名）	zìxíngchē	2-8
自由	（形）	zìyóu	3-2
自由泳	（名）	zìyóuyǒng	3-2
字	（名）	zì	3-2
综合	（动）	zōnghé	4-3
综合课	（名）	zōnghékè	4-3
总	（副）	zǒng	5-1
总是	（副）	zǒngshì	5-1
总之	（连）	zǒngzhī	6-7
粽子	（名）	zòngzi	6-1
走	（动）	zǒu	1-9
走廊	（名）	zǒuláng	6-9
租	（动）	zū	6-3
足迹	（名）	zújì	4-3
足球	（名）	zúqiú	3-1
组织	（动）	zǔzhī	5-2
嘴唇	（名）	zuǐchún	6-3
最	（副）	zuì	1-5
最好	（副）	zuìhǎo	2-3
最近	（名）	zuìjìn	1-5
尊敬	（动、形）	zūnjìng	6-5
遵守	（动）	zūnshǒu	4-9
昨天	（名）	zuótiān	1-9
左	（名）	zuǒ	2-8
左边	（名）	zuǒbian	2-8
左面	（名）	zuǒmiàn	4-2
作业	（名）	zuòyè	1-5

作用	（名）	zuòyòng	6-6
坐	（动）	zuò	2-7
座	（量）	zuò	2-8
座位	（名）	zuòwèi	5-6
做	（动）	zuò	1-5
做法	（名）	zuòfa	6-10
做客	（动）	zuòkè	4-2
做梦	（动）	zuòmèng	4-7
做主	（动）	zuòzhǔ	4-8

专名　Proper nouns

A		
阿虎	Ā Hǔ	5-9
阿拉伯文	Ālābówén	2-4
阿拉伯语	Ālābóyǔ	2-4
阿龙	Ā Lóng	5-9
埃及	Āijí	4-3
艾米	Àimǐ	1-2
安徽	Ānhuī	6-7
安娜	Ānnà	6-9
澳大利亚	Àodàlìyà	4-3
B		
八达岭	Bādá Lǐng	5-5
白华	Bái Huá	1-1
北海	Běihǎi	3-7
北京	Běijīng	2-4
北京大学	Běijīng Dàxué	5-3
北京饭店	Běijīng Fàndiàn	6-2
北京外国语大学	Běijīng Wàiguóyǔ Dàxué	6-3
北京晚报	Běijīng Wǎnbào	4-2
贝拉	Bèilā	2-1
彼得	Bǐdé	2-5
C		
长城	Chángchéng	4-3
嫦娥	Cháng'é	5-4
嫦娥奔月	Cháng'é bēn yuè	5-4
陈红	Chén Hóng	5-7
陈文山	Chén Wénshān	4-1
川	Chuān	4-5
春节	Chūnjié	5-4
春秋	Chūnqiū	5-5
D		
大连	Dàlián	3-1
大内上子	Dànèi Shàngzǐ	1-2
大同	Dàtóng	6-8
大雁塔	Dàyàn Tǎ	6-3
大洋洲	Dàyángzhōu	4-3
德文	Déwén	2-4
德语	Déyǔ	2-4
滴滴	Dīdī	6-2
丁	Dīng	2-4
丁兰	Dīng Lán	1-9
端午节	Duānwǔjié	5-4

E		
俄文	Éwén	2-4
俄语	Éyǔ	2-4
F		
法文	Fǎwén	2-4
法语	Fǎyǔ	2-4
方龙	Fāng Lóng	1-1
方云天	Fāng Yúntiān	1-8
非洲	Fēizhōu	4-3
费城	Fèichéng	6-3
福建	Fújiàn	6-7
复兴门	Fùxīng Mén	4-9
G		
高	Gāo	3-4
高敏	Gāo Mǐn	4-9
高山	Gāo Shān	5-1
高英	Gāo Yīng	4-1
故宫	Gùgōng	4-3
广东	Guǎngdōng	4-5
广州	Guǎngzhōu	3-1
桂林	Guìlín	4-3
国庆节	Guóqìngjié	6-8
H		
哈尔滨	Hā'ěrbīn	5-3
海伦	Hǎilún	2-1
韩国	Hánguó	2-5
汉日词典	Hàn-Rì Cídiǎn	2-2
汉英词典	Hàn-Yīng Cídiǎn	2-2
汉语	Hànyǔ	1-8
汉语水平考试	Hànyǔ Shuǐpíng Kǎoshì	4-2
汉字	Hànzì	1-5
杭州	Hángzhōu	3-1
和平路	Hépíng Lù	6-2
和平门	Hépíng Mén	4-9
红娘	Hóngniáng	5-1
虎跑泉	Hǔpǎo Quán	6-7
虎山	Hǔ Shān	5-5
怀特	Huáitè	3-6
黄河	Huáng Hé	5-3
黄山	Huáng Shān	6-7
火把节	Huǒbǎjié	5-4
J		
吉姆	Jímǔ	6-4
加利福尼亚	Jiālìfúníyà	6-3
加拿大	Jiānádà	4-3
嘉峪关	Jiāyù Guān	5-5
金汉成	Jīn Hànchéng	1-2
旧金山	Jiùjīnshān	6-3
K		
可口可乐	Kěkǒu-kělè	1-3
孔鲤	Kǒng Lǐ	6-5
孔子	Kǒngzǐ	6-5
昆明湖	Kūnmíng Hú	4-3
L		
老舍	Lǎo Shě	6-7
李	Lǐ	2-4
李逵探母	Lǐ Kuí Tàn Mǔ	5-7
立春	Lìchūn	4-7
立秋	Lìqiū	4-7
林明	Lín Míng	5-8
刘	Liú	3-4
刘江	Liú Jiāng	4-9
卢京生	Lú Jīngshēng	6-10

鲁	Lǔ	4-5
M		
马	Mǎ	2-4
马可·波罗	Mǎkě Bōluó	4-3
玛丽	Mǎlì	3-6
美国	Měiguó	1-3
美洲	Měizhōu	4-3
明（朝）	Míng (cháo)	6-6
明代	Míngdài	5-5
N		
南京	Nánjīng	3-1
内蒙古	Nèiměnggǔ	6-7
纽约	Niǔyuē	6-3
O		
欧洲	Ōuzhōu	4-5
Q		
钱	Qián	3-9
钱塘江	Qiántáng Jiāng	6-3
秦朝	Qíncháo	5-5
秦始皇	Qín Shǐhuáng	5-5
青岛	Qīngdǎo	3-1
清（朝）	Qīng(cháo)	6-6
清明节	Qīngmíngjié	5-4
R		
人民日报	Rénmín Rìbào	4-2
日本	Rìběn	1-8
日汉词典	Rì-Hàn Cídiǎn	2-2
日文	Rìwén	1-8
日语	Rìyǔ	1-8
S		
山本正	Shānběn Zhèng	1-2
山东	Shāndōng	4-5
山西	Shānxī	6-8
上帝	Shàngdì	6-9
上海	Shànghǎi	2-10
圣诞节	Shèngdànjié	5-4
世界公园	Shìjiè Gōngyuán	4-3
水上公园	Shuǐshàng Gōngyuán	4-3
四川	Sìchuān	4-5
四郎探母	Sìláng Tàn Mǔ	5-7
宋大江	Sòng Dàjiāng	5-7
宋英	Sòng Yīng	6-8
苏州	Sūzhōu	3-9
孙	Sūn	3-9
T		
泰国	Tàiguó	6-7
天安门	Tiān'ān Mén	5-5
天津	Tiānjīn	3-1
吐鲁番	Tǔlǔfān	6-8
W		
王才	Wáng Cái	1-7
王欢	Wáng Huān	1-4
王小康	Wáng Xiǎokāng	6-5
王学艺	Wáng Xuéyì	6-5
王志强	Wáng Zhìqiáng	6-5
吴	Wú	3-9
武汉	Wǔhàn	5-3
武周山	Wǔzhōu Shān	6-8
X		
西安	Xī'ān	3-1
西班牙文	Xībānyáwén	2-4
西班牙语	Xībānyáyǔ	2-4
西藏	Xīzàng	6-7

西湖	Xī Hú	4-3
西直门	Xīzhí Mén	4-9
希尔顿饭店	Xī’ěrdùn Fàndiàn	6-10
香山	Xiāng Shān	3-6
新疆	Xīnjiāng	4-3
徐春兰	Xú Chūnlán	6-2
Y		
亚洲	Yàzhōu	4-3
杨静	Yáng Jìng	4-7
依丽拉	Yīlìlā	6-8
颐和园	Yíhé Yuán	3-7
意大利	Yìdàlì	2-5
意大利文	Yìdàlìwén	2-4
意大利语	Yìdàlìyǔ	2-4
英国	Yīngguó	6-4
英汉词典	Yīng-Hàn Cídiǎn	2-2
英文	Yīngwén	2-4
英语	Yīngyǔ	2-4
于	Yú	2-4
元朝	Yuáncháo	6-6

元宵节	Yuánxiāojié	5-4
云冈石窟	Yúngāng Shíkū	6-8
云南	Yúnnán	6-7
Z		
张	Zhāng	2-4
赵	Zhào	2-4
赵林	Zhào Lín	2-10
郑	Zhèng	3-9
支付宝	Zhīfùbǎo	2-3
中国	Zhōngguó	1-4
《中国民俗研究》	《Zhōngguó Mínsú Yánjiū》	5-2
《中国文化研究》	《Zhōngguó Wénhuà Yánjiū》	3-6
中华人民共和国	Zhōnghuá Rénmín Gònghéguó	6-8
中秋节	Zhōngqiūjié	5-3
中文	Zhōngwén	1-6
周	Zhōu	3-9
周小芳	Zhōu Xiǎofāng	5-1
朱佳	Zhū Jiā	6-2

Key to exercises and homework
课堂练习和家庭作业参考答案

第一课

三、课堂练习

（二）词语

从本课生词表中选择合适的词语填空

（1）我今年在初级汉语班学习，明年去中级汉语班。

（2）山本正汉字写得非常工整。

（3）这种药很有效，我吃了三次感冒就好了。

（4）丁兰做什么事儿都非常认真，从来不马虎。

（5）表里所有的栏目都要填写清楚。

（6）这本书的封面设计得很好。

（7）你不是申请继续学习吗？办手续了吗？

（8）王才说的笑话真逗，把所有的人都逗笑了。

（9）政府制定了有关外国留学生的法律。

（10）警察把事情的经过调查清楚了，他们写了一份调查报告。

（11）老师是从事教育工作的人。

（12）他在大学学的是汉语专业。

（13）老师和学生必须互相合作，共同努力，才能搞好教学。

（14）我哥哥快结婚了，我未来的嫂子是小张的姐姐。

（15）安娜的父亲曾经是美国驻华大使。她毕业后也想当外交官。

（16）这本教材是新出版的，很受学生欢迎。

（17）多学习一些知识就多了一份资本，更容易找到工作。

（18）艾米把那束鲜花插在花瓶里了。

（19）小王和小李已经订婚了，但还没结婚。

(20) 这张名单怎么没有我的名字?

(21) 从小学升入中学不用经过考试。

(22) 你选谁当先进教师?

(23) 金汉成说:"现在学习汉语，是为了将来跟中国做生意。"

(24) 我们一起建设美好的未来。

(三) 句型

2. 判断下列反问句的本意（表示肯定时，在括号里画✓；表示否定时，在括号里画×）

(1) 不请假，合适吗? (×)

(2) 换个班学习，还要填申请表吗? (×)

(3) 这么简单的道理，你也不懂吗? (✓)

(4) 有人打搅你，你高兴吗? (×)

(5) 我跟谁一起出去的，你不是看见了吗? (✓)

(6) 这么近，还用骑车吗? (×)

(7) 你不是喜欢这个专业吗? 为什么说这个专业不好? (✓)

(8) 他给我们介绍经验! 他干过这个工作吗? (×)

(9) 你不是有个朋友在驻华使馆工作吗? 你去请他帮个忙。 (✓)

(10) 你不是想当外交官吗? 你应该了解各国情况。 (✓)

(11) 不学好知识，怎么能建设自己的国家? (×)

(12) 你不是想学习西方先进的科学技术吗? 将来去美国留学吧。 (✓)

四、家庭作业

(一) 阅读

1. 选择正确答案

(1) B　　(2) A　　(3) D　　(4) C

（二）词语

2. 用“至于”完成句子

（1）我只知道这个星期的活动计划，至于明天的安排还要问一下。

（2）我们都想去桂林旅行，至于能不能去还要看领导的决定。

（3）我认为事实是这样，至于是不是这样还需要去调查。

（4）他们来这里主要是调查问题，至于什么时候有结果还不清楚。

（5）小王过生日，我们决定为他点一首歌，至于送什么礼物还在商量。

（6）这个月我们办公室必须有一个人出差，至于谁去要开会来决定。

第二课

三、课堂练习

（二）词语

从本课生词表中选择合适的词语填空

（1）小王昨天半夜从歌厅回来。

（2）我们这次去杭州旅行住的是小旅馆，很便宜。

（3）今天刚25号，这个月的工资我都花光了。

（4）你怎么天天加班，回来得这么晚？

（5）山本的嫂子是家庭妇女，每天买菜做饭，照顾丈夫和孩子。

（6）这台新设备是进口的，那条自动生产线也是从国外引进的。

（7）工人们正在安装机器。

（8）别把纸片扔在地上。

（9）我怎么能扔下工作去看电影呢？

（10）这是一张空头支票，银行不付款。

（11）安娜顺利地通过了这次考试。

（12）这个戒指是不是金的？请你鉴定一下。

（13）这里是新技术开发区，有很多研究项目。

（14）经理正在跟外商洽谈生意。

（15）这个星期我天天在家里接待客人。

（16）小张和小李在工作上互相支持，他们是一对好夫妻。

（17）这么多家务活儿全落在她一个人的肩上。

（18）那辆车很空，咱们坐那辆吧。

（19）我站在你的背后，你没看见。

（20）我只在乎质量，至于价钱多少我不在乎。

（21）老刘很少说话，他总是默默地工作。

（22）他的一生都奉献给了国家的教育事业。

（23）你看，5号运动员冲到了最前边。

（24）今天太晚了，明天我再跟你算账。

（25）那个孩子骗老师，装作肚子疼的样子。

（26）他怎么总是重复一个句子？他不会说别的吗？

（27）要处理好问题，先得进行调查分析。

（28）年轻人要努力学习科学知识，将来更好地建设自己的祖国。

（三）句型

2. 给下列陈述句加上合适的句尾语气助词

（1）哦，是王秘书哇。

（2）到时候，我会通知你的。

（3）他这是空头支票哇。

（4）鉴定会下午两点才开始呢。

（5）我们公司也想开发新产品哪。

（6）我应该受罚，我骑车带人了嘛。

（7）他当然会成功了，背后有个默默奉献的妻子嘛。

（8）今天加班要加到半夜呢。

（9）这不说明问题呀。

（10）我让他来，他不来呀。

四、家庭作业

（一）阅读

1. 读下面的对话并填空

夫妻对话

赵　林：（敲门）哎，杨静，开门哪！

杨　静：谁呀？半夜三更的敲门！

赵　林：连我的声音都听不出来了？我是赵林。

杨　静：是你呀，我还以为是坏人呢，你回来干什么？

赵　林：睡觉呗。都半夜了，我还没吃饭呢。

杨　静：还没吃饭？我才不信呢，经理没请你吃饭？

赵　林：真的没吃饭，骗你不是人。

杨　静：你要是不饿不困就不回家了，是不是？赵大工程师，我这儿是旅馆还是饭店？我是你的保姆还是服务员？

赵　林：杨静！

杨　静：别叫，叫也没有用！今天本旅馆不营业，本饭店不开张！

赵　林：咳，杨静，到月底了，公司里特别忙。那么多工作，我能扔下不管吗？再说，也不是我一个人加班呀，所有的技术人员都刚刚回家，连领导也刚刚回家。

杨　静：天天忙，月月忙，你哪天正点下过班？这些日子家里的事儿你问过吗？买粮买菜、洗衣做饭、接送孩子，全成了我的事儿。我不是家庭妇女，我也有自己的工作！

赵　林：杨静，别嚷嚷了，让邻居听见多不好。以后我多干点儿，不行吗？

杨　静：你还怕人听见？我偏要嚷。经理把你当成大红人，产量上不去找你，自动线坏了找你，设备安装也找你，可怎么不问问你肚子饿不饿？

赵　林：杨静，先开开门，咱们屋里说，行吗？

杨　静：想进家门，没那么容易！

赵　林：那我走了。杨静，明天我早点儿下班，路上我买菜，晚饭我做。

杨　静：站住！你去哪儿？

赵　林：回单位睡觉。

杨　静：你不饿了？

赵　林：饿一顿没关系。

杨　静：回来！你以为一走就没事儿啦？没那么简单，进屋来再和你算账……先去吃饭吧，饭菜在电饭锅里热着呢。

（三）句型

把下列反问句改写成相应的陈述句

（1）哦，你还有回来早的时候？

你从来没有回来早的时候。

（2）都这么晚了，他还没吃晚饭？

都这么晚了，他应该吃了晚饭了。

（3）这本教材是你的？你仔细看看！

这本教材不是你的。你仔细看看！

（4）你工作这么积极，经理没请你吃饭？

你工作这么积极，经理应该请你吃饭。

（5）你还怕人听见？

你不应该怕人听见。

（6）这种事儿还能开玩笑？

这种事儿不能开玩笑。

（7）他半年都没逛过商场？不太可能吧！

他不太可能半年没逛过商场。

（8）不给他加班费，他也不在乎？

不给他加班费，他不会不在乎。

（9）你要是不饿不困，就不回家了？

你不饿不困也应该回家。

（10）他们那儿是农业大国，还缺粮食？

他们那儿是农业大国，不应该缺粮食。

第三课

三、课堂练习

（二）词语

1. 从本课生词表中选择合适的词语填空

（1）与其求别人不如求自己。

（2）招待会结束以后，他们立刻返回了学校。

（3）这个话剧表现了年轻人的爱情生活。

（4）求职者要学会推销自己。

（5）有的年轻人喜欢去外国独资企业或者中外合资企业求职。

（6）这么好的机会你为什么放弃呢？

（7）我有能力做好这个工作。

（8）昨天我们参观了一家公司，这家公司的经理是个难得的人才。

（9）王老师专门负责培训工程师。

（10）我决定明年报考北京大学。

（11）他的学历是大学本科，他想今年报考研究生。

（12）他们毕业以前要先去医院实习，实习合格以后才能当医生。

（13）小周太骄傲了，她以为自己比其他同学考得好。

（14）我们单位今年招来了一些高层次、高水平的博士研究生。

（15）很多农村的年轻人向往城市生活。

（16）这几天我太忙了，明天的宴会我恐怕去不了。

（17）有的人过分热情，让人觉得不太舒服。

（18）你们有什么意见可以大胆地提。

（19）王老师的介绍促使我下决心去吐鲁番旅行。

（20）前三次试验都失败了，第四次成功了。

（21）每个人都有长处和短处。

（22）社会上的人际关系比学校里复杂。

（23）你能不能把你们的计划详细地谈谈？

(24) 根据你说的情况，他们一定是误解你了。

(25) 他们说的上海话连南方人都听不懂，何况外国人呢？

(26) 现在市场上的商品非常丰富，想买什么就能买什么。

(27) 我们公司新来的公关经理很有才能。

2. 连线

与其找个不理想的工作，	不如求自己。
与其当翻译，	不如坐飞机去。
与其求别人，	不如当老师。
与其买这件衣服，	不如去西安旅行。
与其去大同旅行，	不如继续学习。
与其坐火车去，	不如买那件衣服。

3. 用下列短语填空

甚至不该说的也说　　　　甚至不真实

甚至该说的也不说　　　　甚至连我

甚至连星期日

(1) 说话过分夸张，甚至不真实，别人就不相信了。

(2) 写文章过分详细，甚至不该说的也说，让人不想看；过分简单，甚至该说的也不说，又让人看不明白。

(3) 他最近非常忙，甚至连星期日也不能休息。

(4) 她说得太快了，甚至连我也听不懂。

（三）句型

2. 把下列反问句改写成相应的陈述句

(1) 在公司工作，哪能不注意人际关系呢？

在公司工作应该注意人际关系。

(2) 你根据什么说他不会推销自己？他早找到工作了！

你没有根据不要说他不会推销自己，他早找到工作了！

(3) 谁说我们公司要招聘新职员？没有的事儿！

我们公司没有招聘新职员的事儿。

（4）那些年纪比你大得多，而且已经有了工作的人还想继续学习，更何况你大学刚刚毕业呢？

你大学刚刚毕业更应该继续学习，那些年纪比你大得多，而且已经有了工作的人还想继续学习呢。

（5）当服务员有什么不好？这也是工作需要嘛。

当服务员很好，这也是工作需要嘛。

（6）我只是个本科毕业生，算什么人才？

我只是个本科毕业生，不算什么人才。

（7）外贸公司有什么可向往的？

外贸公司没有什么可向往的。

（8）这哪是他的长处？

这不是他的长处。

（9）有意见就提，这有什么过分的？

有意见就提，这没有什么过分的。

（10）他的层次高什么？

他的层次不高。

3. 把下列陈述句改写成特指问形式的反问句

（1）他并不骄傲。

他有什么可骄傲的？

（2）他工作不够大胆。

谁说他工作很大胆？

（3）他算不上人才。

他算什么人才？

（4）他的工作表现不太好。

谁说他的工作表现好？

（5）他介绍得不太详细。

谁说他介绍得很详细？

（6）这点儿钱恐怕不够用。

这点儿钱怎么够用？

（7）他们都不想报考研究生。

谁说他们都想报考研究生？

（8）我没有放弃这个想法。

我怎么能放弃这个想法呢？

（9）我这样说并不过分。

我这样说有什么过分？

（10）我不想搞外贸。

我为什么要搞外贸？

四、家庭作业

（二）词语

2. 用“尽管”完成句子

（1）你们有什么意见尽管提。

（2）你们有什么问题尽管问。

（3）需要我帮忙，请尽管说。

（4）尽管不喜欢去，我们还是去了。

（5）尽管没有做过，但我可以试试。

（6）尽管想了很多办法，问题还是没有解决。

第四课

三、课堂练习

（二）词语

从本课生词表中选择合适的词语填空

（1）河水受到污染，河里的鱼都死了。

（2）张老师研究教学法，写了不少文章，取得很多成果。

（3）赵林他们为了开发新产品不知付出了多少心血。

（4）切菜的时候要小心，别切了手。

（5）秋天是收获的季节。

（6）妈妈从冰箱里拿出来一些饮料。

（7）那个孩子得了肠炎，又吐又泻，被送到了医院。

（8）祝你一路平安！

（9）老师向同学们宣布："这次考试艾米荣获全班第一名"。

（10）他们两个对这件事儿的看法完全相反，一个说好，一个说不好。

（11）校长讲完话以后同学们热烈鼓掌。

（12）在口语课上，老师让同学们做会话／对话练习。

（13）贝拉向老师和全班同学汇报旅行的经过。

（14）别担心，他不会有危险的。

（15）这里的气候很好，冬天不冷，夏天不热。

（16）这些孩子乐于助人，多么可爱啊！

（17）他的劲儿真大，能举起100公斤的东西。

（18）这个秘密我决不告诉别人。

（19）那两个演员说的相声真逗。

（20）听说母亲得了癌症，小刘急哭了。

（21）小宋和小林打算旅行结婚，不举行婚礼了。

（22）在晚会上，老师和同学们表演了丰富多彩的文艺节目。

（23）课后，学校为同学们组织了很多娱乐活动。

（三）句型

2. 给下列感叹句加上合适的句尾语气助词

（1）这个相声说得真好哇！

（2）现在是收获的时候啦！

（3）这多么危险哪！

（4）这里的气候条件多好啊！

（5）这多让人担心哪！

（6）礼堂里的喝彩声、欢呼声多大呀！

（7）他的劲儿多大呀！

(8) 这个教堂多高哇！

(9) 马上就要宣布评选结果啦！

(10) 我的钱剩得不多啦！

第五课

三、课堂练习

（二）词语

从本课生词表中选择合适的词语填空

(1) 这个工厂的厂长姓付，书记姓郑。

(2) 服务员把咖啡放在每个人的面前。

(3) 茶几上摆着漂亮的茶具。这些茶具都是瓷的，做得非常精致。

(4) 我完全能体会你现在的心情，我一个月没收到信，也很着急。

(5) 小孙感冒了，症状是头疼、嗓子疼、鼻子不通、四肢无力。

(6) 从这儿到剧场比较远，走路至少得用20分钟。

(7) 难怪贝拉今天这么高兴，原来口语考试她得了第一名。

(8) 小王得了肠炎，又吐又泻，难受极了，赶快打电话叫急救车吧。

(9) 赵林他们在极其困难的情况下进行试验，实在不容易。

(10) 那个孩子太懒，从来不帮父母做家务。

(11) 这篇文章的内容极其深刻，人们从中可以悟出很多道理。

(12) 今天的练习他做了整整两个小时。

(13) 这条路虽然远一点儿，可是路很平，司机们都愿意走这条路。

(14) 到底行还是不行，请你给我一个确定的回答。

(15) 考试的时间已经确定了，在下个月5号。

(16) 他们今天干喝酒，不吃菜。

(17) 老吴写了一份深刻的检讨书，检讨了自己不重视安全生产的错误。

(18) 金汉成是一个篮球运动员，他投球很准。

(19) 你说他偷了你的钱包，有什么证据？

(20) 听说儿子偷了别人的东西，老张气得要命。

(21) 谢谢您为我们准备了丰盛的晚餐。

(22) 这次试验的材料你带来了吗？

(23) 他们没有理解老师的用意。

(24) 你别装模作样了，我们知道这件事儿是你干的。

(25) 这些青年人非常努力，进步很快。

(26) 你怎么没参加毕业典礼？

(27) 艾米的记忆力很强，这些生词她看一遍就能记住。

(28) 那位年轻的记者写了一篇很长的文章，深刻地批评了某些人大吃大喝的问题。

（三）句型

2. 给下列祈使句加上合适的句尾语气助词

(1) 你可不能这么懒哪！

(2) 出发的日期，你得早点儿确定下来呀！

(3) 你给大家谈谈体会吧！

(4) 我们可不能大吃大喝啊！

(5) 你可要清白地做人哪！

(6) 这封信，你要早点儿寄出去啊！

(7) 你要深刻地检讨自己呀！

(8) 你别装模作样啦！

(9) 我们可不能让他销毁证据呀！

(10) 你别干喝酒哇！

第六课

三、课堂练习

（二）词语

1. 从本课生词表中选择合适的词语填空

(1) 想不出更好的解决办法，我很苦恼。

(2) 现在的电视节目广告太多。

(3) 小王的听力不太好，他感到学习很吃力。

(4) 太胖的人容易得心脏病。

(5) 一年来，小冯学习努力，进步显著。

(6) 这个节目吸引了很多观众。

(7) 这种方法省力气，可是费材料。

(8) 饭菜已经凉了，我给你热热吧。

(9) 星期日他照例六点起床，然后去操场跑步。

(10) 把衣服扣子扣上吧，外边有点儿凉。

(11) 他总是在背后议论别人。

(12) 请打开书，看73页倒数第5行。

(13) 今天早上我只喝了一碗粥。

(14) 那位老人拖着沉重的双腿走上楼梯。

(15) 孩子们都爱吃巧克力。

(16) 在公共汽车上，一个人踩了我的脚，他说："对不起！"我说："没关系！"

(17) 孩子们一边拍手，一边唱歌。

(18) 下了课，请你立即到我的办公室来，我告诉你一个重要的消息。

(19) 赵林想，哪怕今天晚上不睡觉，也要把试验做完。

(20) 这是国家的政策，我们不能改变。

(21) 孩子喜欢就让他去学吧，别限制他。

(22) 别灰心，坚持下去，一定会成功的！

(23) 那个孩子没做作业，挨了老师的批评。

(24) 单位进口了一些新式设备。

(25) 女儿累瘦了，妈妈很心疼她，每天给她做很多好吃的。

(26) 电灯是一个叫爱迪生的美国人发明的。

(27) 这个楼的电梯又坏了，我们只好爬楼梯了。

(28) 张老师的夫人是护士，在第三医院工作。

（29）我的腰今天有点儿疼，我想去医院看看。

（30）这么简单的问题他竟回答不出来，真是没想到。

2. 把下列短语扩展成句子

（1）回答得很干脆

大内回答得很干脆。

（2）做事儿干脆得很

金汉成做事儿干脆得很。

（3）都很干脆

贝拉和艾米都很干脆。

（4）干脆跟你说

我干脆跟你说吧。

（5）干脆不承认

他干脆不承认。

（三）句型

2. 完成句子

（1）他一边捂着肚子，一边对医生说。

（2）他一边上楼梯，一边打电话。

（3）他一边吃着巧克力，一边看电视。

（4）他一边慢慢地跑步，一边听音乐。

（5）他一边走，一边唱。

（6）他一面工作，一面学习。

（7）他一面劳动，一面读书。

（8）他一面学习，一面搞发明。

（9）他一面做生意，一面搞设计。

（10）他一面搞外贸工作，一面搞生产。

四、家庭作业

（二）词语

2. 用“不然”完成句子

（1）快起来吧，不然就迟到了。

（2）咱们坐出租车去吧，不然就来不及了。

（3）你得参加这次考试，不然没有成绩。

（4）他得了心脏病，得立即送医院，不然非常危险。

（5）去东北旅行一定要多穿衣服，不然会感冒的。

（6）你们一定要预习听力课的生词，不然听不懂课文。

3. 用“反而”完成句子

（1）我原来想，走这条路近，没想到反而远了。

（2）我以为把这个消息告诉她，她一定很高兴，可她反而生气了。

（3）他每天都来得很早，今天考试，他反而来晚了。

（4）现在是春天了，这几天反而冷了。

（5）又学了半年汉语，他的口语不但没有提高，反而不如以前了。

（6）老张说雨快停了，过了一个钟头，雨不但没停，反而更大了。

第七课

三、课堂练习

（二）词语

从本课生词表中选择合适的词语填空

（1）今天，我们在这里设宴，为张先生接风／送行。

（2）老校长为教育事业奋斗了一生。

（3）分别多年的老朋友今天团聚了。

（4）小英去美国以后嫁给一位华侨的儿子。

（5）我有一桩心愿没有了却。

（6）礼物很轻，但这是我们大家的一片心意，请你一定收下。

(7) 结婚五十周年是金婚。

(8) 我始终不明白他为什么不喜欢他父亲。

(9) 刘教授退休以后创建了一所语言学校。

(10) 刚到日本，我们的生活非常艰苦，每天晚上要去公司或饭馆儿打工。

(11) 那位老人临死的时候把他要说的话说尽了。

(12) 经过反复练习，才能记住这些词的意思和用法。

(13) 小刚从来不说假话，他是个诚实的孩子。

(14) 你是什么时候取得博士学位的？

(15) 妈妈把全部时间和精力花在孩子身上，她要把孩子培养成一个优秀的电影演员。

(16) 快走吧，不然就赶不上火车了。

(17) 那位海员的手指接上以后，非常灵活，现在写字、打字都没有问题。

(18) 谦虚是一种美德。

(19) 女儿得了癌症，妈妈的心情十分悲痛。

(20) 那个女孩儿继承了父亲的聪明和母亲的美丽。

(21) 这位老华侨始终思念／想念祖国和祖国的亲人。

(22) 刚来到中国的时候，艾米非常想念／思念她的爸爸和妈妈。

(23) 母亲是个勤劳的人，她每天从早忙到晚。

(24) 他从小就非常勇敢，不怕任何困难。

(25) 听了这个好消息，大家都十分欢喜。

(26) 老牛凭着丰富的工作经验当上了经理。

(27) 小张年轻，头脑灵活，办事又很认真，所以领导很喜欢他。

(28) 公司创建的时候，规模很小，现在已经有两千多职员了。

(29) 战争结束以后，这个国家很快富强起来了。

(30) 昨天上午学校举行了隆重的开学典礼。

(31) 玛丽明天回国，今天晚上我们请她吃全聚德的烤鸭，为她送行。

（32）我要为家乡的建设尽一份力。

（三）句型

2. 从下列句子中挑选出可变换为“既……又……”和“又是……又是……”格式的句子

（1）这个人又吹牛，又骗人。

这个人既是吹牛，又是骗人。

这个人又是吹牛，又是骗人。

（2）孩子做错了事儿，他又打又骂。

孩子做错了事儿，他既是打又是骂。

孩子做错了事儿，他又是打又是骂。

（3）他又懂业务，又有事业心。

他既懂业务，又有事业心。

（4）这地方又干净，又安静。

这地方既干净，又安静。

（5）你这样说，又对又不对。

你这样说，既对又不对。

（6）她见到分别多年的弟弟，心里又高兴，又难过。

她见到分别多年的弟弟，心里既是高兴，又是难过。

她见到分别多年的弟弟，心里又是高兴，又是难过。

（7）亲人团聚，全家又高兴又激动。

亲人团聚，全家既高兴又激动。

（8）他又有工作经验，又有工作热情。

他既有工作经验，又有工作热情。

（9）他又可能去颐和园，又可能去故宫。

他既可能去颐和园，又可能去故宫。

（10）他又头脑灵活，又有艰苦奋斗的精神。

他既头脑灵活，又有艰苦奋斗的精神。

（11）这个工厂规模又大，设备又全。

这个工厂既规模大，又设备全。

(12) 这个人又干坏事，又怕别人知道。

这个人既干坏事，又怕别人知道。

第八课

三、课堂练习

(二) 词语

1. 从本课生词表中选择合适的词语填空

(1) 上海队经过努力奋斗，终于取得了胜利。

(2) 这家商店主要经营服装和鞋帽。

(3) 我本来不想去，后来他们都劝我，我只好去了。

(4) 我们班的同学多数会说英语，只有两个人不会。

(5) 近几年，这里新建了许多大商场，成了一个新的商业中心。

(6) 这些建筑设计新颖，十分美观。

(7) 这件衣服的款式不错，做工也很精细。

(8) 这是大商场，不是个体小商店。

(9) 这些服装是从法国进口的高级时装，价钱都很贵。

(10) 饭馆儿的墙上有一块牌子，牌子上写着四个大字："宾至如归"。

(11) 这些孩子以前对客人没有礼貌，现在变得非常文明了。

(12) 你觉得这个城市怎么样？

(13) 别犹豫了，赶快决定吧。

(14) 总经理打电话询问我的意见。

(15) 上课的时候，同学们都主动回答老师的问题。

(16) 在医生和护士的精心照顾下，我很快恢复了健康。

(17) 艾米花了10000美元买了一幅十分名贵的中国画儿。

(18) 这次机会很难得，千万不要失去。

(19) 天快黑了，前边的山和树都变得模糊了。

(20) 你现在不同意，当初为什么不说？

(21) 改革经济，对外开放，使这里的市场越来越兴旺繁荣。

(22) 那位年轻的女售货员说话和气，对顾客非常热情。

(23) 你不是拿不定主意买什么礼物吗？请白老师给你出谋划策吧。

2. 从下列词语中选择合适的填空

来自　选自　出自　寄自　译自

(1) 这篇文章选自《人民日报》。

(2) 我们班有的同学来自亚洲，有的来自欧洲，有的来自美洲。

(3) 这封信寄自上海。

(4) 这些工艺品都出自那位老人之手。

(5) 这个词译自德语。

（三）句型

2. 完成句子

(1) 学习外语，一方面要听，一方面要说。

(2) 记忆生词，一方面要记，一方面要念。

(3) 外出旅游，一方面要欣赏美景，一方面要品尝美食。

(4) 买东西，一方面要看价格，一方面要看质量。

(5) 星期天，他有时候去商店，有时候去看电影。

(6) 这几天，他有时候去图书馆看书，有时候在家搞设计。

(7) 这几个月，他有时候去外地出差，有时候在单位加班。

(8) 这几年，他有时候在北京教学生，有时候去国外参加学术会议。

(9) 这孩子好动，一会儿玩儿电脑，一会儿玩儿游戏。

(10) 他感冒了，一会儿咳嗽，一会儿流鼻涕。

(11) 他没有一定的主意，一会儿想去，一会儿不想去。

(12) 那里的天气不正常，一会儿下雨，一会儿刮风。

四、家庭作业

（二）词语

2. 用“繁荣”完成句子

(1) 我们的国家越来越繁荣富强了。

(2) 改革开放以后，市场经济更加繁荣了。

(3) 我的故乡变得更繁荣、更美丽了。

(4) 这个城市优美的环境、繁荣的经济给我留下了深刻的印象。

(5) 我们要努力让经济更繁荣，提高人民的生活水平。

3. 用“也许”改写句子

(1) 天这么晚了，她可能不来了。

天这么晚了，她也许不来了。

(2) 我们很多年没有联系，恐怕他早把我忘了。

我们很多年没有联系，也许他早把我忘了。

(3) 金汉成大概明年暑假回国。

金汉成也许明年暑假回国。

(4) 走这条路可能近一点儿。

走这条路也许近一点儿。

(5) 你去帮他恐怕更好一点儿。

你去帮他也许更好一点儿。

第九课

三、课堂练习

(二) 词语

从本课生词表中选择合适的词语填空

(1) 快到寒假了，今年寒假我和全家人准备去山上滑雪。

(2) 你闻闻，这是什么味儿？

(3) 一下雨，这里到处是污水，可臭了。

(4) 这条河的上游有好几个工厂，污染了河水，下游的老百姓连喝水都有了困难。

(5) 这个国家以前很乱，现在治理得真不错。

(6) 王欢回到故乡，乡亲们都来看他。

(7) 我们的院长刚刚上任，他还不太了解情况。

(8) 一日之计在于晨，一年之计在于春。

(9) 小田的老家在农村，不在城市。

(10) 我们要互相关心、互相照顾，不能只顾自己的利益，不顾别人的利益。

(11) 这里是中国最大的工业区。

(12) 你找的人远在天边，近在眼前。

(13) 经过努力，他们的理想变成了现实。

(14) 回国以前，我跟老师和同学们告别。

(15) 学校为同学们的生活和学习提供了很多方便的条件。

(16) 为了把问题搞清楚，必须做彻底的调查。

(17) 他仅仅用了半个钟头就做完了试验。

(18) 保护环境，努力平衡人类和大自然之间的关系，每个人都有责任。

(19) 那些孩子很聪明，能明白老师的意思。

(20) 由于改革开放，这个国家的经济得到迅速的发展。

(21) 不能只顾眼前，你有没有一个长远计划？

(22) 地球是人类生活的空间。

(23) 经过论证，这个计划半年就能实现。

(24) 这个地区还没开发，大森林里有许多珍贵的动物。

(25) 这个地区经济的发展不平衡，有的地方比较先进，有的地方比较落后。

(26) 这个县的工业发展很快，可是农业还比较落后。

(27) 环境污染威胁着人类的生存。

(28) 这次去桂林，公司为职员提供了旅游的经费。

(三) 句型

2. 选词填空

还　　再　　更　　并且　　特别是

(1) 丁兰会跳舞，还能教跳舞。

(2) 我喜欢动物，特别是喜欢熊猫。

(3) 彼得已经去过三次长城了，他想今年暑假再去一次。

(4) 艾米除了学习汉语，还学习日语。

(5) 贝拉喜欢打球，还喜欢打太极拳。

(6) 汉语很难，特别是汉字。

(7) 我们班的同学都参加了汉语水平考试，并且取得了很好的成绩。

(8) 我已经学了汉语、日语，明年开始再学一门韩国语。

(9) 我们在北京游览了长城、故宫，还吃了烤鸭、看了京剧。

(10) 我喜欢夏天，更喜欢秋天，因为秋天是收获的季节。

四、家庭作业

(一) 阅读

1. 连线

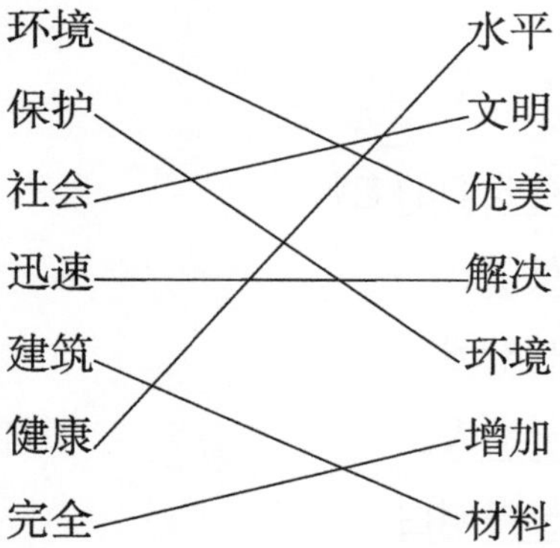

(二) 词语

2. 用下列词语完成句子

顾

(1) 大家都不喜欢那个年轻人，他只顾自己，不顾别人。

(2) 老张要求自己很严格，他一生都是只顾他人，不顾自己。

(3) 我们要为子孙后代造福，不能只顾眼前利益，不顾长远利益。

(4) 昨天下午我只顾写文章，忘了去开会。

(5) 这么多事情，你一个人顾得过来吗？

(6) 小陈奋不顾身，从火里救出一个孩子。

宁 可

(1) 我宁可不睡，也要把这些事情做完。

(2) 他们宁可不挣钱，也不污染环境。

(3) 艾米宁可在家，也不跟贝拉一起来。

(4) 母亲宁可不买米，也要给孩子买那件生日礼物。

告 别

(1) 你别送了，咱们就在这儿告别吧。

(2) 王欢告别了故乡，又回到北京。

(3) 你怎么没跟老师告别？

(4) 我跟她告别的时候，她哭了。

(5) 我没想到那么多人来跟我告别。

（三）句型

完成句子

(1) 我不但会唱歌，还会跳舞。

(2) 他不但是我们的朋友，还是我们的老师。

(3) 他不但会说汉语，还会说英语。

(4) 贝拉不但喜欢游泳，还喜欢滑冰。

(5) 王才不但努力学习，还乐于助人。

(6) 我们不但看得清楚，还能想得明白。

(7) 这个练习很难，不但学生不会做，老师也不会做。

(8) 不但年轻人喜欢这个运动，老人和孩子也喜欢这个运动。

(9) 不但小孩子喜欢熊猫，成年人也喜欢熊猫。

(10) 不但妻子做家务活儿，丈夫也帮着一起做家务活儿。

(11) 这里的环境不错，不但学习环境很好，老师们也非常优秀。

(12) 这个地区污染很严重，不但河水污染了，土地也不能种粮食了。

第十课

三、课堂练习

（二）词语

从本课生词表中选择合适的词语填空

（1）我去机场迎接一个美国艺术代表团。

（2）你的房间布置得真不错。

（3）他的生活习惯很特殊，跟别人都不一样。

（4）山本非常大方，跟朋友出去总是他花钱。

（5）这个建筑又大方又典雅。

（6）大内靠在沙发上睡着了。

（7）赵林靠自己的努力当上了工程师。

（8）中国总理首先举行欢迎仪式，随后两国总理举行了正式会谈。

（9）新郎身穿笔挺的西装，新娘穿着白色婚纱，他们照了一张相。

（10）别干那种费力不讨好的事儿。

（11）那个小伙子很会讨好领导，别人都看不起他。

（12）晚会结束了，同学们纷纷走出礼堂。

（13）天气太热，他们带的食品都变质了。

（14）政府要坚持反对腐败。

（15）那个老人的右眼瞎了。

（16）说话得有证据，不能瞎说。

（17）我的头发太长了，该理发了。

（18）上学期我们开了两次座谈会，讨论学习方法问题。

（19）总理正在做政府工作报告。

（20）我们敬爱的孙校长退休了。

（21）这次贸易会谈非常成功，一共签订了10项合作项目。

（22）校长先总结了上学期的工作，紧接着又布置了本学期的工作。

（23）客人们祝新郎新娘的美好姻缘天长地久。

（三）句型

2. 用“以后”“后来”“接着”“随后”“又”“再”填空

（1）他是前年调到我校来的，后来走了。

（2）你回国以后，有空儿给我来封信。

（3）我明天去故宫，后天再去颐和园。

（4）他做完作业以后，又看了一会儿电视。

（5）我发完言了，你接着发言吧。

（6）开始我和安娜在一个班，后来她去外交学院了。

（7）他昨天进了一趟城，今天又进了一趟城。

（8）你别急，这件事儿我以后再告诉你。

（9）你先走，我随后就到。

Index of grammar (Volume 2—Volume 7)
语法索引（第2册—第7册）